Contents

Reflective exercises

JO FINCH

SUPPORTING STRUGGLING STUDENTS ON PLACEMENT

A practical guide

 ORTS POLICY & PRACTICE

First published in Great Britain in 2017 by

Policy Press
University of Bristol
1-9 Old Park Hill
Bristol
BS2 8BB
UK
+44 (0)117 954 5940
pp-info@bristol.ac.uk
www.policypress.co.uk

North America office:
Policy Press
c/o The University of Chicago Press
1427 East 60th Street
Chicago, IL 60637, USA
t: +1 773 702 7700
f: +1 773 702 9756
sales@press.uchicago.edu
www.press.uchicago.edu

British Library Cataloguing in Publication Data
A catalogue record for this book is available from the British Library.

Library of Congress Cataloging-in-Publication Data
A catalog record for this book has been requested.

ISBN 978-1-4473-2873-5 (paperback)
ISBN 978-1-4473-2875-9 (ePub)
ISBN 978-1-4473-2876-6 (Mobi)
ISBN 978-1-4473-2874-2 (ePdf)

Cover design by Policy Press
Front cover: image kindly supplied by Shutterstock
Printed and bound in Great Britain by CMP, Poole
Policy Press uses environmentally responsible print partners

Acknowledgements

I would like to thank practice and field educators everywhere, who continue to work with students in challenging circumstances, that is in an environment of reduced budgets and raised thresholds, and in a culture of a lack acknowledgment and appreciation by employers (and sometimes university staff) of the important and complex work they do with students from many professions. Many practice educators worldwide do not receive payment for the work they do and without this voluntary and often unappreciated contribution practice educators make to their professions, there would be serious shortages of qualified professionals in many occupations.

In terms of social work practice educators, I would like to thank those I have met in the many presentations and workshops on struggling and failing students I have delivered all over the UK for their engagement and commitment to upholding standards in social work. The lively debates that often follow these sessions are always helpful and constructive, and have afforded me the opportunity to develop my ideas further. In particular I would like to thank and express my sincere gratitude to the practice educators who work with University of East London social work students, often taking on the role with positivity and enthusiasm, despite increasingly complex and demanding workloads.

Thanks to Edith Akinnawonu, for always asking if I had finished yet. Huge thanks go to my two BFFs Pam Whittingham and Jane

Haluwa and social work educator buddies Siobhan Maclean, Prospera Tedam, Kim Detjen and David McKendrick for unwavering support and encouragement. Prospera Tedam in particular went way beyond the call of duty, demanding updates on the percentage of words I had written, refusing to put up with my lame excuses and for engaging with me in weekend WhatsApp 'write-offs'.

Huge thanks and appreciation are also due to the publishers, who put up with my failing academic ways in terms of my inability to meet several deadlines. In no way is this a good example to set to students.

Last but not least, big thanks and appreciation to my family, who continue to support me in untold ways, including the many hours of free childcare given over the years by both sets of grandparents (Jean, Tony, Val and Jim). Much love and appreciation to my partner, Simon, and my sons, Louis and William, for, as always, helping me keep it all in perspective.

INTRODUCTION

Practice education for the most part is a rewarding and positive experience. In a former role as a practice educator, students were often the 'nice' part of my job, given that my social work role often involved undertaking complex parenting assessments for the family courts. The students I worked with in that particular agency were highly motivated, enthusiastic, had up-to-date knowledge, lacked cynicism and offered in return a critical but constructive view of the agency, its policies and procedures. Most importantly, they also provided a much-needed reminder of why I had entered social work in the first place. It is inevitable, however, that some students will not live up to expectations for a variety of reasons. There is also a minority of students who will not be able to meet the requirements of the profession, and so during placement it will fall to practice educators first, to do all they can to support those students to make the necessary development and second, if required, to fail students, following due process. This is the practice educator's ultimate role – to act as a gatekeeper to the profession – and, as the book goes on to document, the gatekeeper role is not without its inherent tensions.

The genesis of the book

This book has emerged from a number of professional experiences spanning almost 20 years. As a social work practitioner working in London in the late 1990s, I was concerned about the competence, conduct and behaviour displayed by some social workers, as well as other professionals. I often thought, 'Who let that one through?'.

There is one case I vividly recall, when I was working for a charity that undertook, among other things, assessments of parents for court proceedings. The local authority social worker in this case was facilitating overnight unsupervised contact for three children placed in voluntary care (Section 20 of the Children Act 1989) with their mother. It was clear that the mother was unable to provide the most basic physical care and there were significant risks in this arrangement that the social worker seemed unable to acknowledge. I distinctly recall at the time wondering how this social worker had been able to pass her social work programme, and in particular, how she had managed the placement components of her course. She appeared cut off emotionally; for example, she responded in a concerning manner to an incident where I was assaulted by the mother, and more importantly, did not seem to understand or consider the significant risks the mother posed to the children in terms of not being able to meet their most basic physical care needs, let alone their safety and emotional needs. Indeed, this was such a powerful experience that even now I question how she had passed the placements on her qualifying programme.

Around the same time as working with this individual, I became a practice educator, and, while on the whole the experience was very positive and included working with some fantastically motivated, enthusiastic and creative social work students, I was involved in a situation as an offsite practice educator where I had to fail a student on their placement. I noted the intense guilt I felt, and the array of challenging and contradictory emotions that emerged so powerfully. I recall a strong gut feeling that somehow this student did not have the 'robustness' or 'personality' for social work, which felt really subjective, judgemental and somewhat at odds with social work values.

In 2002, I moved from practice to the academy, teaching on a pre-qualifying social work programme (at the time, a Diploma in Social Work), and it became apparent that failing students, both students failing academically and especially those on placement, appeared to provoke intense feelings in everyone, that is tutors, students and practice educators. In the first year of my lecturing career, I came across a practice educator who failed a student on what I felt were

2

very dubious and oppressive grounds, for example, criticising her West African pronunciation of 'foyer'. I was really pleased when the student went on to pass a further placement but remained concerned about the conduct of the practice educator and the implications for his practice as a social worker. He subsequently moved to another borough.

In that first, challenging year of teaching, I struggled to make sense of my social work tutor role and found situations of students failing on placement difficult, not least that uncomfortable sense of being caught between two, often cross and angry people. Namely the student and the practice educator, both with often very different perspectives on what had happened. I noticed further examples of practice educators who appeared to be unable to recognise serious concerns about the performance and conduct of the student placed with them. Social work tutors also seemed to find it difficult to accept that a student was failing, and, in one worrying example, appeared to put pressure on a practice educator to pass a student about whom there were some significant concerns. In 2003, I was fortunate to be in a position to explore my concerns, experiences and interests further when I enrolled on a part-time professional doctorate in social work at the University of Sussex. My thesis consequently explored the experiences of practice educators who had worked with a struggling or failing student, although not all had gone on to fail the student at the end of the placement. At that time, there was little interest, either academically or practically, from a UK social work perspective about students failing in placement, and so for the doctorate I drew on research from international and comparator professions. It was notable that many professions with assessed periods of learning in the field experienced the same issues, concerns and dilemmas.

The issue of failing students, however, did not go away for me after completing the doctorate. First, it was an inevitable feature of my role as a social work lecturer and programme leader of an MA in social work that I was supporting students who had failed either academic modules or their placement; second, as the current module leader for the Stage Two Practice Educators Professional Standards, I support practice educators through the challenges of working with students, a minority of whom may well be struggling; third, in my role as a social work tutor, I am required to liaise with tutees and practice educators; and fourth, I have maintained my research interests in practice education and learning, and indeed I have been able to extend and develop my work further – much of which is reported in this book.

I was very influenced in the initial stages of my doctoral research (and still am) by an early, but still pertinent, article by Brandon and Davies (1979) that sets out many of the existing debates today about practice learning, its complexities and its challenges. The authors maintain that focusing on failing students provides a way of interrogating the issues, debates, challenges and dilemmas inherent in practice learning and assessment more generally, as the complexities come to the fore sharply and decisively in failing situations. My aim for this book, however, is not just on the management of struggling or failing students in a constructive and confident way, but on how to develop and improve practice education with *all* students in practice settings from both social work and kindred disciplines.

It is pleasing to note that academics and practitioners, from social work and other professions, have continued to undertake research in practice education, as well as focus on the issues raised by marginal, struggling or failing students. This is a hopeful sign of the increased recognition of the 'field' as a valuable and important site of study in itself; for example, it can often reveal something important about the nature, culture and 'under-the-surface' features of the profession itself, as well as its importance for students training to become qualified in their particular professions.

Concerns about practice learning

Practice learning is often taken for granted in many professions' training requirements and it seems both obvious and common sense that students need an opportunity to apply what they have learnt in the classroom setting in a practical context, responding to real-life issues and people with complex needs, often in challenging circumstances. Students also need to practise the skills of navigating (and surviving) the confusing and bewildering world of organisations as well as working across organisations with professionals who may hold very different values. It is now unthinkable that students with only a theoretical knowledge would be considered safe to practice. Indeed, some Canadian social work academics have gone as far as arguing that field education is the signature pedagogy of social work (Wayne et al, 2013).

While the importance and centrality of practice learning to social work and other professions is not in dispute, in the UK at least some persistent concerns have arisen about practice learning. In brief, these centre on three main issues:

- the quantity and quality of placements (Kearney, 2003; Phillipson, 2006; Croisdale-Appleby, 2014);
- the perception of low failure rates (SWRB, 2010);
- the reluctance of practice educators to fail students. (Coulshed, 1980; Shapton, 2006; Finch and Taylor, 2013)

Terminology

The terminology used throughout this book relates to terms used in the English social work education context. Practice educator is used to denote the qualified professional who assesses and supports trainee professionals in placement. Practice educators are often known as mentors in nursing education, supervisors in clinical psychology and field educators in North American and Australian social work contexts.

Practice education and practice learning are used interchangeably, and describe the overall phenomenon of supporting and assessing would-be professionals or students in practice situations. In North American and Antipodean social work contexts, this would largely be known as field education. In the UK social work context, the placement itself is known in a variety of ways, including the placement or the practice learning setting. These terms will be used interchangeably and describe what is often known as the 'practicum' in

North American contexts or the field placement. In other professions, the practicum might also be referred to as the clinical placement.

The term university tutor used here is more commonly known as faculty liaison in North American contexts, and refers to the representative from the university who would attend placement meetings to ensure that the student is receiving appropriate learning opportunities.

Struggling, marginal, borderline or failing?

It has always been somewhat of a dilemma deciding which terms to utilise to denote a student who might be experiencing difficulties on placement, or who may be struggling to meet professional requirements. The term 'marginal' was originally used by Brandon and Davies (1979) and might now be considered somewhat at odds with social work values.

In psychology, counselling and psychotherapy, terms such as 'impairment' (Elman and Forest, 2007) and 'competence problems' (Forest et al, 2008) are commonly used, and in nursing the phrase 'the underachieving learner' (Anglia Ruskin University, 2013) makes an appearance. The discomfort in describing some students in such a negative way is explored in Chapter Three, which considers the emotional challenges that can arise in such situations. Clearly at this point we can see some of the challenges of the social work practice educator role, especially when the profession internationally holds a belief in people's capacity to change (Reamer, 2006; Bisman, 2014). In my research work to date, I have used the somewhat loose terms 'struggling' or 'failing', but, as I go on to discuss in this book, such terms can be problematic and can potentially label the student in unhelpful and disempowering ways.

Aims and scope of the book

The book is primarily centred on social work practice education in a UK context, but has relevance for professions internationally, where there are requirements for an assessed period of practice in the field. This includes, for example, nursing, teaching, osteopathy, physiotherapy, counselling psychology and occupational therapy, to name but a few of the professions that require assessed learning in a practice situation. While the book's main aim is to consider the issues of working positively with students in the field who may have temporary or more substantial difficulties to overcome in meeting the requirements of social work, the issues raised in the book have relevance for work with all students in a field or clinical placement. The book's main audience is practice educators and aims to offer a useful mix of the existing research as well as practical ways forward. The style of the book is very much informal, while maintaining an appropriate, but nevertheless accessible, academic tone. My aim therefore, is to aid practice educators to think further about the application of theoretical concepts to their work, as well as provide some practical strategies for managing students who are struggling to meet requirements.

The book has also been written with university tutors in mind, as universities are part of the system that contributes to, and makes decisions about, students passing or not passing their placement. As such, those comprising the 'learning team' around the student need to work together in a positive way, as explored further in Chapter Five.

All chapters identify a number of key texts that explore the phenomenon under discussion. Pedagogical features include case vignettes and reflective exercises to promote critical reflection. Overall, the book's intention is to offer a practical and theoretical guide to working positively with struggling or failing students, and provide practice educators and university tutors with critical thinking tools, to understand their own and the students' emotional states, and, if necessary, fail students in a safe, fair, transparent and confident manner.

Chapter One explores practice learning and assessment across professions and considers the history of practice learning within social work education. The chapter details the reforms that have taken place in the UK in the past decade or so in terms of social work education. The concerns and challenges that have been raised about practice learning in the research literature are also considered, and include a discussion about the role of the practice educator and the claim that there is a 'fail to fail'.

Chapter Two details the behaviours, traits or issues displayed by students that are possible indications that they are struggling or at risk of failing. The chapter explores the challenges around this and the possible adverse impact of labelling on a student's ability to be open to learning. The chapter uses a range of theoretical perspectives to explore why some students may find it challenging to learn. The chapter further explores the challenges around identifying a struggling or failing student and urges caution about the uncritical adoption of the trait approach in doing so. The chapter thus considers the difference between a short-term block to learning and something much more substantial and concerning. The chapter also details concerns about discrimination in practice education.

Chapter Three focuses on the emotional impact of working with a struggling or failing student in a practice learning setting. The chapter begins with a reflective exercise that focuses on our own experiences of failing. The chapter outlines research studies that highlight the uncomfortable and difficult emotional responses that may emerge when practice educators are confronted with a struggling or failing student. Possible explanations for such emotional processes are explored through a range of theories, such as transactional analysis, Karpman's drama triangle and projective identification. Overall, the chapter encourages a reflective approach to the task of practice education and the emotional dynamics that forcibly come to the fore when a student is struggling or failing their placement.

Chapter Four considers the most effective strategies for managing and working positively with students experiencing difficulties in placement. It considers choice of assessment strategy, teaching and learning input, initial judgements made about the student, and ways of clarifying both expectations and the role of the practice educator. This chapter in particular documents research that explores practice educators who are able to fail students without distressing levels of emotionality and considers the strategies they use. The chapter also covers issues such as the fair assessment of students and positive, non-discriminatory ways of working.

Chapter Five explores relationships between the field and the academy and highlights research that documents the difficult blaming relationships that can sometimes emerge. The chapter considers the reasons for this and offers practical ways forward for practice educators to work constructively with the university. The chapter also focuses on the role of university tutors in supporting practice educators to work with all students.

The concluding chapter draws out the main themes emerging from the book and offers a summary of the practical ways forward in managing struggling or failing students. The chapter offers some final comments about the challenges of assessing practice. The implications for other related contexts, for example supervision and management, are also considered briefly. The book ends by concluding how important it is to fail a student if required, ensuring that the failure is a 'good one'.

1
THE CONTEXT OF PRACTICE LEARNING AND ASSESSMENT ACROSS PROFESSIONS

It's very easy to pass a student but very, very difficult to fail a student. (Duffy, 2003, p 38)

Introduction

This chapter discusses practice education generally and considers its relevance and importance to a wide range of professions that involve assessed periods of practice. It focuses specifically on practice education in relation to social work in the UK, considers the history of practice learning as well as detailing the numerous reviews and developments in social work education. The chapter offers a critical exploration of the impact of continuous reform, not least in terms of its impact on practice learning. It then moves on to consider the nature of practice learning and the multifaceted role of the practice educator that makes the task complex. Despite the centrality of practice learning in many professions, however, both the various reviews into social work in particular and the international research across professions in general highlight persistent concerns and complexities associated with practice learning and assessment, and the chapter explores these concerns and challenges. Lastly, the chapter critically considers the 'failure to fail' contention that is particularly prevalent in nursing and social work, but also appears in other professions.

The importance of practice learning

Assessed periods of learning in the field are common in social work throughout the world, as well as in many other cognate professions (Hughes and Heycox, 1996; Raymond, 2000; Doel and Shardlow, 2002). Practice placements provide students or trainees the opportunity to put into effect what they have learnt in an academic context (Evans, 1999; Furness and Gilligan, 2004). It is the place where theory and practice interact and synergise. It is also the site where concerns about someone's competence, capability and suitability for the profession are thoroughly tested (Finch and Poletti, 2013). It is therefore a major site of gatekeeping, to ensure that those who have failed to reach the minimum standards, who are not capable, or even dangerous, do not go on to become qualified practitioners (Lafrance et al, 2004). Practice educators' ultimate responsibility of course, is to service users or patients, and to prevent possible future harm, by not assessing as competent a student who is not yet ready to qualify. Indeed, an article by a group of 'experts by experience' of health and social care services in the UK, makes this point, namely that users and patients will ultimately '... bear the ramifications' (Malihi-Shoja et al, 2012, p 10) of poor practice education. As a member of the writing group comments:

> "As a service user/carer, I have in the past felt let down by a social worker who I did not think should be doing this as a job! And it made me think about how did the social worker not get the advice needed to do this job in the first place?" (Malihi-Shoja et al, 2012, p 13)

Of course gatekeeping and the protection of service users is not the sole domain of practice educators, as all stakeholders, particularly universities and their tutors, also have gatekeeping responsibilities relating to their professional values and ethical codes of conduct, and this is explored in Chapter Five.

Developments in social work education

There have been significant policy and practice developments in social work education in the UK, not all of which have been welcomed by the profession. These are important in understanding the current situation, in England especially, which at the time of writing was still undergoing uncertainty and change. Social work education, in comparison with other professions with assessed learning requirements, is subject to constant development and it is worth considering why this is so.

The view that social work requires academic learning was established in the UK in the late 19th century with the rise of Charity Organisation Society (COS) volunteers – the 'social workers' of the time. Indeed, Parrott (1999) argues that it is generally agreed that formalised social work education in the UK began in 1896 with a series of lectures designed for COS volunteers. In 1903, a School of Sociology and Social Economics was established in London (Powell, 2001), and at the same time a School of Social Science was set up in Liverpool (Lyons, 1999). In 1912, the School of Sociology and Social Economics became part of the Department of Social Policy and Administration under the auspices of the London School of Economics and Political Science (LSE) (Lyons, 1999). The department is still in existence today at the LSE, but the last cohort of trainee social workers was admitted to the MSc and Diploma in Social Work programme in 1995, qualifying in 1997 (Finch, 2005).

In the 1920s, other social work programmes were developed, including those at Barnett House in Oxford (now part of Oxford University) and Bedford College in London (now part of Royal Holloway, University of London). The establishment of these colleges was prompted by general concerns for social welfare, by reform promoting women's participation in education, and by reform in higher education in general. Indeed, the founders of Barnett House were also part of the settlement movement and the college was subsequently set up to 'advance the systematic study of current social and economic questions, to encourage and train people to take up social and caring work, particularly in the urban "settlements" in disadvantaged areas, and to promote adult education' (www.spi.ox.ac.uk/about-us/history.html).

Such programmes offered teaching 'on a range of academic and professional subjects … and students spent an equivalent time in practical work' (Lyons, 1999, p 6). The practice placement therefore became established at the very beginning of formalised professional training in social work. The 1940s to 1960s were a time of consolidation in the development of social work training within universities, which, as Lyons (1999) argued, peaked in the 1960s with the expansion of higher education more generally and the development of non-graduate routes into social work training. In 1971, the Central Council for Education and Training in Social Work (CCETSW) replaced the Council for Training in Social Work (Sawdon, 1986) and the Certificate in Qualified Social Work (CQSW) was established along with four routes for entry into social work: non-graduate, undergraduate, postgraduate diploma and master's levels (Finch, 2005).

An alternative social work qualification, the Certificate in Social Services (CSS), was introduced in 1975 because of 'dissatisfaction with the CQSW' (Lyons, 1999, pp 11-12). Colleges and employers subsequently offered the CSS. A division began to emerge, however, in that CQSW became the qualification gained by those in front-line social work and the CSS by those working in residential and daycare settings (Finch, 2005). In 1984, a plan was proposed for an additional third year of training but the Conservative government of the time rejected this on the basis of cost (Lyons, 1999). In 1989, CCETSW argued the case for one single award, the Diploma in Social Work (DipSW), to replace the former awards in 1995 (CCETSW, 1989; Sharp and Danbury, 1999). Lyons (1999) argued that the Diploma in Social Work represented the 'dominance of political and employer influence over professional interests' (Lyons, 1999, p 15). A competency approach was therefore introduced, with students assessed against key roles. The competency approach to professional education more generally has been criticised on a number of grounds, not least that it artificially simplifies complex professional skills, knowledge and processes into discrete units of tasks, and serves only to encourage a tick-box approach to the task of assessment (Eraut, 1994; Owens, 1995; O'Hagan, 1996; Parrott, 1999). Further concerns have centred on the incompatibility between anti-discriminatory principles and practices with competency approaches (Jayaratne et al, 1992; Brummer, 1998; Cowburn et al, 2000) and on the view that a focus on behavioural outcomes devalues the reflective learning process, which is rendered inconsequential to the final outcome (Cowburn et al, 2000; Humphrey, 2007).

Of direct relevance to the substantive topic of this book, namely students struggling to meet the requirements, Sharp and Danbury (1999) argued that the development of the Diploma in Social Work centred on concerns about the low failure rate of the CQSW, which was seen as 'evidence of low standards in student selection and poor assessments that led to students passing who should not' (1999, p 5). Sharp and Danbury (1999) also argued that further impetus for change included child abuse cases leading to public inquiries in which social service departments and social workers were highly criticised, and the concern that the CQSW was no longer relevant, given changing priorities within social service departments and new ways of service delivery. The competing needs and priorities of the profession, the universities and employers were, and remain, a source of tension, and these tensions are often evident, either explicitly or inexplicitly in professional training requirements. Indeed, Chapter Six explores some of these tensions and dilemmas in more detail, particularly in terms of how such tensions affect the relationships between workers in the field and the academy.

In 2003, the degree in social work was introduced in England (2004 in Wales, Scotland and Northern Ireland) and would replace the Diploma in Social Work. The move to a degree was prompted by a number of considerations, bringing the qualification requirement up to a comparable educational level to other similar professions, such as nursing and teaching, in the hope that it would increase public trust and confidence in the profession and transform its status (Department of Health, 2004; Orme et al, 2009).

This also coincided with the introduction of the Care Standards Act (2000), which ensured that regulatory bodies for social work education and practice were set up in each of the four countries in the UK, the General Social Care Council (England), the Scottish Social Services Council, the Care Council of Wales and the Northern Ireland Care Council. 'Social worker' became a registered title under the Act, so only those registered with a care council could work in a designated social work role (Finch and Taylor, 2013). Moreover, to call oneself a 'social worker' without being registered with one of the four care councils became a criminal offence (McLaughlin, 2008). As part of their remit, the care councils were tasked with regulating social work education, and a tribunal system was established to manage social workers and student social workers who were deemed to have breached their professional codes. Indeed, the first General Social Care Council tribunal hearing was held in April 2007, and centred on the case of a social worker who was also working as an escort (Currer and Atherton, 2008). The social worker was subsequently suspended from the register for two years (McLaughlin, 2008).

The main features of the new degree in social work included a curriculum that followed Department of Health (DH) guidelines, an increase in the amount of time spent in assessed placements from 130 to 200 days, and more stringent entrance requirements and suitability processes for candidacy for social work programmes (DH, 2002; Finch and Taylor, 2013). Service users and carers were also required to take an active role in all aspects of programme design and delivery (Finch and Taylor, 2013). As part of these developments, practice learning was given more status on programmes, with fifty percent of courses spent on practice learning (more for those undertaking the postgraduate route into social work). Placements providers were also, for the first time, provided with funds to support students via educational support grants, and students in all of the four countries within the UK were assessed against newly developed National Occupational Standards for Social Work (TOPSS, 2002).

Practice education developments

At the time of the CQSW and CSS qualifications, practice supervisors, as practice educators were known then, were required to have been qualified for two years and to have attended a non-assessed introductory course (Sharp and Danbury, 1999). A criticism of the model was that practice supervisors appeared to carry little influence in the final decision making about a student's competence and safety to practice (Brandon and Davies, 1979; Sharp and Danbury, 1999). As such, decisions about a student's performance on placement was tutor-dominated (Sharp and Danbury, 1999).

The DipSW required practice supervisors to undertake the Practice Teaching Award. Practice supervisors became 'practice teachers', with the aim of emphasising the teaching aspect of the role. As discussed earlier, concerns were raised about the competency model approach to the task of assessing professionals in practice learning settings. Indeed, Cowburn et al (2000) made the important point that inherent in competency models is the concept of the assessor as neutral. They argue:

> … the assessor is effectively an intellect, divorced from identity, gender, race, class and culture, who can provide a value-free, assessment of the student's performance. (Cowburn et al, 2000, p 631)

This is very important in the context of this book, which focuses on the emotional aspects that makes the assessment of professionals in practice so complex, as well as the very real concerns about the limits of a competency approach to the task of assessing practice. The introduction of the degree in social work saw the practice teacher become the 'practice assessor' and at the time of writing the term 'practice educator' was well established in the UK.

In 2007, post-qualifying frameworks were developed, with three awards available at specialist, higher specialist and advanced levels, which equated to a graduate diploma, postgraduate diploma and master's-level award (Finch, 2010). This development was led by the regulatory body for social work in England, the General Social Care Council (GSCC). The Practice Teaching Award was scrapped, and practice education qualifications were available at higher specialist and advanced levels only. Such awards – usually stand-alone, 30-credit modules – emphasised enabling the learning of others (Finch, 2010).

Further social work education developments

One event that had a significant impact on social work education concerned the death of a 17-month-old toddler, Peter Connelly, in Haringey, North London. Baby P, as he was initially known, died at the hands of his mother, his mother's partner and the partner's brother in 2007. The case became the subject of a media storm in 2009 after the criminal trial was concluded. The child had been known to a range of services prior to his death, and at postmortem was found to have sustained 50 previous injuries. As a result of an intense media, public and political outcry – in part because the London Borough of Haringey had previously experienced another high-profile child abuse death, that of Victoria Climbié in 2003, for which social workers were publically held to blame – the Labour government set up a Social Work Task Force (SWTF) to explore both front-line children and family social work and by implication social work education. The SWTF therefore made a number of observations and recommendations. Of direct relevance to social work education and by implication practice learning and assessment, the SWTF's interim report criticised social work education. Indeed, in its interim report, *Facing up to the Task* (2009), the following strong statement was made:

> Specific concerns have been raised about the ... robustness and quality of assessment, with some students passing the social work degree who are not competent or suitable to practise on the frontline. (SWTF, 2009, p 24)

One recommendation from the task force was to set up a Social Work Reform Board to oversee future developments. As part of this, a College of Social Work was proposed, which would aim to promote social work, improve public understanding of social work and promote best practice in an attempt to 'drive up standards' (UK Parliament, 2012). The college was duly set up, and hopes were high that there would be positive change.

While the Social Work Reform Board was finalising its report, Eileen Munro, a professor of social work at the LSE, was tasked by the then Conservative-Liberal coalition government in June 2010 to review child protection services and practices, which culminated in a series of reports (Munro, 2010, 2011a, 2011b). In short, Munro advocated a more intuitive approach to social work practice and she was critical of the managerial approach that had emerged in social work practice, namely the strict adherence to computer-monitored timescales, which led to a range of unintended consequences for practice that were felt to be highly detrimental to service users, including deskilling and de-professionalisation among social workers rather than enhanced practice wisdom and confidence.

Hopes were high in the profession that a reduced reliance on new public management approaches, and a return to more intuitive and relationship-based approaches to practice, alongside the establishment of the College of Social Work (TCSW), would herald a new era of social work practice in England. A further significant development, led by TCSW, was the move away from a competency model of placement assessment, namely the occupational standards for social work that were applicable in England at that time, to a capability framework known as the Professional Capability Framework (PCF). The PCF was intended to follow practitioners from entry on to a social work programme, through assessed readiness for practice, to two placements and an assessed and supported year in employment with a clear career progression route. It is also worth noting that in 2012, the General Social Care Council was abolished and its regulatory functions taken over by the Health Professions Council, which subsequently became the Health Care Professions Council (HCPC). This immediately put social work in England on a different regulatory footing from that in other countries in the UK, which retained their original regulatory bodies set up under the Care Act (2000) and maintained a competency approach to assessing students in placement. As part of this development in England, the post-qualifying frameworks ceased to be subject to regulatory control and have been somewhat adrift ever since. Furthermore, students could not be registered with the HCPC, unlike their counterparts in Northern Ireland, Wales and Scotland.

Of direct relevance to practice learning and assessment, TCSW also developed the Practice Educators' Professional Standards. From 2013, practice educators were required to undertake a stage 1 and stage 2 practice educators' programme and only those with a stage 2 qualification were able to assess final placement students, supervise and assess approved mental health practitioner trainees, or work as mentors/assessors for the recently introduced Assessed and Supported Year in Employment for newly qualified social workers.

This period of optimism in social work in the UK and particularly England began to be undermined, in my opinion, by two further government-commissioned reports into social work, this time with a distinct focus on social work education. Professor Croisdale-Appleby, a health specialist, was commissioned by the Department of Health in 2014. This was followed two weeks later by the appointment of Sir Martin Narey, formerly a civil servant in the prison service and latterly the chief executive of a children's charity, by the Department of Education, also to undertake a review of social work education. Coming after the many changes and developments since the 1980s, these further reviews, undertaken by people outside of the profession, were felt to be somewhat politically inspired, confusing and not exactly neutral (see, for example, Cleary, 2014; Bamford, 2015). In brief, Narey was highly critical of current social work education, and advocated a move towards specialist training, rather than the current generic model with specialist training occurring at post-qualifying levels. Narey was also critical of the complicated regulatory framework, namely the HCPC standards of proficiencies and the College of Social Work's requirements regarding the PCF. Narey's report however, was widely criticised for its weak methodological approach (Schraer, date unknown). Croisdale-Appleby's report was more methodologically robust (Cleary, 2014) and advocated only postgraduate routes into social work training. Both reports were critical of current placement provision, with Narey commenting that voluntary agency placements were not adequately preparing students for the task of statutory social work, and Croisdale-Appleby arguing that there needed to be more alignment between numbers of students on social work programmes and local workforce development needs, as well as raising some concern about the quality of placements. At the time of writing, the government was considering developing a new regulatory body in social work in England, which, as a matter of concern, will not be an independent body but will come under direct government control. Alongside the rather surreptitious introduction of the Chief Social Workers' Knowledge and Skills Statements (one set for work with children and families and one set for work with adults), which are already in operation in terms of the assessed and supported year in employment, the current model against which social work practice is assessed, at both qualifying and post-qualifying levels, remains unclear in England.

Given the long and complicated history of social work in the UK, with growing differences between the countries of the UK, also perhaps promoted by devolution in the UK more generally, the numerous reviews and the almost continuous state of flux, it is worth taking stock and reflecting on the impact of so many reforms. One of the key issues is that practice educators may well be assessing students using a different assessment system from the one against which they were assessed. Moreover, as a practice educator you might be working with a student who is working towards an academic qualification that is higher than the one you have achieved as a result of the changing nature of the social work qualifications over the years. This may raise another unintentional dynamic.

Reflective exercise 1.1: History of your profession

History of social work education	History of other profession's education
Was there anything about the history of social work education in the earlier account that surprised you?	What are the early origins of your profession's training?
What was the model you were assessed against as a student? What do you recall about the model used?	How has the qualification required changed for your profession since its early origins and do you think this is a positive development?
What do you think about the current model of the assessment of social work students on placement (strengths, weaknesses and challenges)?	How has practice or clinical learning been assessed over the years and does it differ from the way you were trained?
Are you confident using the model to assess social work students?	What is your profession's approach to practice learning and assessment?
Is it important that the student placed with you understands the history of social work training?	What are the strengths of this particular approach?
What do you think might be the impact on practice learning given the continuous reforms of social work education?	What are the limitations and challenges of this particular approach?

Concerns about practice learning

A question was raised earlier about why social work, particularly in England, seems to be subject to repeated reviews, and indeed reviews by people outside of the profession, as well as continual changes to the form, content and ways of assessing practice in placement settings. One compelling hypothesis is that social work is perceived by the public as a failing profession because of high-profile child deaths that often highlight shortcomings in individual social workers rather than focusing on structural issues, the realities of identifying risk and the roles of other professionals in the child protection system. A compelling argument put forward by Cooper and Lousada (2005) is that the reason for the intense public outcry at horrific child deaths, often accompanied by political action in the form of reviews, task forces, changes in legislation and the scapegoating of the social work profession, is not so much a failure of social workers to do the task, but rather the failure of social workers to shield and protect the public from the knowledge and realities of horrific child abuse at the hands of parents and carers. My view is that the 'under-the-surface fears of failure' may unconsciously inhabit the practice–educator student relationship, and indeed Chapter Four explores this further. Social work education, as is social work practice, is not politically neutral, and practice educators from all professions are encouraged to take a critical perspective.

There are some positive messages, however, that have arisen from the constant reforms of social work education. First is the growing recognition of the importance and centrality of the practice placement and the attempt to ensure that social work students are assessed using national assessment frameworks, recognising, of course, the different approaches in each of the countries of the UK, namely the National Occupational Standards (NOS) for Social Work in Wales (Care Council for Wales, date unknown) and Northern Ireland, the Standards in Social Work Education in Scotland, which are mapped against the former NOSs (Dunworth and Gordon, 2014). Second is the move towards professionalising and standardising the role of the practice educator via qualification requirements as well as the growing academic research interest in practice learning. Third is the adoption of particular approaches to assessment in placement, which, while offering clarity and uniformity, have undergone some degree of critical scrutiny. For example, the competency approach to the assessment of professionals in practice has long been criticised by a number of social work writers (Jones and Joss, 1995; O'Hagan, 1996; Humphries, 1998; Furness and Gilligan, 2004).

Despite some very positive developments, there have been consistent and long-standing concerns about practice learning and placements, which, notwithstanding the continuous reforms and reviews, keep emerging. These centre on three key areas:

- the quantity and quality of placements in providing appropriate learning opportunities that prepare students for the realities and rigour of qualified practice, particularly in statutory sectors;
- the rarity of placement failure;
- practice educators' apparent reluctance, or inability, to fail students if they need to, in other words, 'failure to fail'.

It is useful now to observe your initial response to the above areas of concern. Do you think these are valid concerns? Have you experienced a poor placement that did not prepare you for the realities of qualified practice? Or perhaps you were concerned that some of your struggling colleagues were passed on your own social work training programme. It is also important to note that practice educators' apparent reluctance to fail is not specific to social work; indeed it arises in other professions with practice learning requirements.

What is practice learning and assessment?

As can be seen, I have somewhat taken for granted throughout this chapter that it is clear what is meant by practice learning and assessment, and, linked to this, the role of the social work practice educator. It is clear that in the UK the role has developed from supervisor to that of teacher, assessor and now educator, which appears to encompass a more holistic approach to the task. The role of the practice educator, however, is far from simple and while there are clear tasks associated with the role, the tasks or functions within the overall role can feel a little contradictory and difficult to reconcile. I would suggest that this role conflict emerges most strongly when a student is struggling to make the necessary progress and development. My doctoral study (Finch, 2010) highlighted the role conflict experienced by some practice educators, in particular an inability to reconcile the nurturer-enabler role of learning with the more managerial, assessor-type role. One practice educator in the study expresses this role conflict really well. She says:

"... there was a clash for me between the facilitator of learning role and the kind of management roles ... now I felt that as a facilitator of learning, I felt very nurturing, especially when a student was clearly evidencing what they were learning and showing that they were enjoying it and saying, 'I enjoy learning' and I respond really well to people who enjoy learning and so there was almost like a maternal feeling about that facilitation of learning but the flip side of that was when I had to become the kind of teller-off or the person who was making judgments about somebody, I did struggle with that ...." (Finch, 2010, p 115)

Field et al (2016) offer a useful account of the myriad of intricate functions inherent in the practice educator role, which reveals all too starkly the complexities and contested nature of the role. They identify the following functions of the practice educator:

- manager;
- enabler of learning;
- facilitator;
- supervisor;
- assessor;
- teacher;
- supporter;
- negotiator;
- planner;
- mediator. (Field et al, 2016, p 10)

Not included in this list, however, are two further crucial roles, namely mentor, and most importantly, gatekeeper to the profession. It is interesting to observe that such an important role – that of gatekeeper – is not included in the above list. This omission was reflected in the research literature that found that practice educators do not explicitly recognise their gatekeeping role (Finch, 2010; Robertson, 2013; Finch and Poletti, 2013). It could be argued that the distinctions between some of these roles might be of a somewhat semantic nature, but it can also be seen how some of the roles might conflict, cause confusion for both practice educators and students alike, and be potentially difficult to reconcile (see, for example, the work of Pritchard, 1995 and Feasey, 2002, on supervisors). As is discussed in Chapter Four, practice educators need to have a clear sense of their roles and responsibilities, and be able to effectively and confidently bring those roles together, which seems to me to mirror the care versus control dilemma inherent in all social work practice. It is worth critically reflecting on all these different aspects within the practice educator role, and to further consider which roles we may feel more comfortable with.

The challenges of assessing practice

If defining and clarifying the myriad and continually shifting roles of a practice educator is challenging enough, not least when particular aspects of the role need to come into play, the complexities of assessing practice, assessment frameworks notwithstanding, is even more exigent. Within social work, this is largely because of the contested notion of what constitutes good enough social work (Lafrance et al, 2004): social work looks different in different agencies, and what is good enough in one agency may not be good enough in another (Sharp and Danbury, 1999; Skinner and Whyte, 2004). Furthermore, one practice educator's standards may not be the same as another's. There is also the associated problem of the alleged gap between being good enough to pass the placement and being good enough to work as a newly qualified social worker (Finch and Taylor, 2012). What is good social work therefore is more generally contested and there will always be a subjective element to the assessment of practice, despite detailed assessment frameworks. The following questions are designed to get you thinking about the challenges of assessing practice in your profession and agency or setting.

Reflective exercise 1.2: Challenges of assessing practice

- What do you find hard or challenging to assess in the students placed with you?
- What do you find easy to assess?
- Why do you think some things are easier to assess than others?
- What do you think are the challenges in assessing practice more generally?
- What are the more general challenges associated with being a practice educator?
- What strategies do you employ to manage these challenges and tensions?

Challenges around assessing practice can therefore include very practical ones, such as increased workloads experienced by front-line professionals, reduced budgets resulting from ongoing economic difficulties, and an accompanying lack of time to undertake the task of practice education effectively. Another challenge might be the lack of acknowledgement of the important role played by social work practice educators in training and supporting the next generation of professionals, from both managers in social work agencies as well as universities. The research from a range of professionals documents the challenges of using the various assessment frameworks effectively (Walker et al, 1995; Hughes and Heycox, 1996) and there are further challenges faced by practice educators in recognising when things are not going as planned or acting in a timely manner to address issues of concern (Duffy, 2004; Kaslow et al, 2007). Another set of challenges revolves around the emotional aspects of assessing practice requirements, as Chapter Three explores in depth. One of the major challenges faced by practice educators, not only from social work but from any profession with assessed practice requirements, concerns working with a struggling or failing student. Associated with this is a concern that there is a 'failure to fail'.

A failure to fail?

As stated at the outset of this chapter, one of the concerns raised across professions with assessed practice requirements is that there is a 'failure to fail'. This implies that practice educators are not failing students who should be failed. As we saw earlier in the discussion of the history of social work education in England, concerns about low failure rates was one rationale for prompting reform in the qualifications. This contention of a failure to fail has been particularly strong in nursing (see, for example, Duffy, 2003; Rutkowski, 2007; Lawson, 2010; Jervis and Tilki, 2011; Larocque and Loyce, 2013), but has also arisen in occupational therapy (Ilott and Murphy, 1997), medical education (Cleland et al, 2005, 2008) and has also found its way into social work (see, for example, Shapton, 2006) in some limited research, but as discussed earlier, appears to have gained uncritical support in various reviews of social work education in the UK.

My position on this issue is that the empirical evidence does not support this hypothesis in a range of professions, and certainly the evidence is not there in terms of social work in the UK. The best we can say is that there is *some* evidence, that *some* practice educators *may* have passed a student who with the benefit of hindsight *may* not have been a clear-cut pass, but we cannot say with certainty what the extent of the problem is. What we can be certain about is that failing a student in a practice learning setting is not a pleasant thing to do, and can cause some practice educators emotional distress. We also know that it also causes university tutors discomfort (see Finch, 2014 and 2016, for example), as well as causing students significant distress (Parker, 2010; Poletti and Anka, 2012). There is more to be gained therefore in understanding why it might be challenging to fail a student in a practice learning setting, and considering the reasons for this using what little empirical evidence there is. In this way, identifying what makes failing a student such a challenging experience can help practice educators in understanding the emotional dynamics at play.

Learning check

- What are three key issues I have learnt from this chapter?
- How do I see my role as a practice educator?
- What roles within the overall role of a practice educator do I feel more comfortable with?
- Why are some roles more uncomfortable than others?

Chapter summary

This chapter has documented the history of social work education in the UK, from its early charitable roots in Victorian Britain to the highly regulated profession it has become today, but a profession that alas still suffers from much public and political condemnation and misunderstanding. The many developments and reviews relating to social work and social work education since 2003 in particular have been both positive and negative. Some developments have been positive, not least the emphasis on the importance of practice learning within qualifying programmes and the need to undertake additional qualifications to become a practice educator. The competency approach, however, to the task of assessing professions (or trainee professionals) has not been without criticism; for example, Cowburn et al (2000) argue that inherent in competency models are positivistic assumptions about the nature of assessment, so the notion that an assessor can be truly neutral and 'an intellect, divorced from identity, gender, race, class and culture, who can provide a "value free" assessment of the student's performance' (2000, p 631) is based on an impossible premise. This then highlights one of the many complexities and challenges faced by professionals when assessing students in placements, and, as part of this complexity, the multifaceted role of the social work practice educator adds dimensions of complication. The chapter lastly explored the 'failure to fail' hypothesis, concluding that there is little empirical evidence to adequately assess the extent of this perceived phenomena. The next chapter goes on to consider what on the surface seems to be a simple and straightforward question: how do we know when a student is failing to achieve the required standards?

Further reading

Doel, M. and Shardlow, S. (2002) 'Introduction: international themes in educating social workers for practice', in S. Shardlow and M. Doel (eds) *Learning to Practise Social Work: International Approaches*, London: Jessica Kingsley Publishers.

Field, P., Jasper, C. and Littler, L. (2016) *Practice Education in Social Work: Achieving Professional Standards* (2nd edn), Northwich: Critical Publishing.

Lyons, K. (1999) *Social Work in Higher Education*, Aldershot: Ashgate.

2

HOW DO WE KNOW WHEN A STUDENT IS FAILING TO ACHIEVE THE REQUIRED STANDARDS?

Interviewer: "What might indicate a student is failing?"
Practice Educator: "I don't know … but I'll know it when I see it … that's a hard question." (Finch, 2010)

Introduction

This chapter considers the challenges around identifying a student struggling or at risk of failing their placement, not least given the varieties of practice and the current tensions in social work, the contested nature of the practice educator role and the lack of a clearly defined standard about what is good enough practice. The chapter considers the difference between a short term, or perhaps temporary, block to learning and something more substantial, longer term and concerning. The chapter then goes on to consider the behaviours and issues that may be indicative of a student struggling or failing. The chapter explores the challenges around this and the possible adverse impact of labelling on a student's ability to be open about their learning needs. It urges caution about a sole reliance on the trait approach to identifying a struggling or failing student and will further consider what it is to fail a placement. The chapter also considers issues around discrimination and prejudice and considers the research that focuses on groups at risk of failure and slow progression.

Learning processes

All students experience challenges and difficulties on placements. Student practitioners, like all of us, learn at different speeds and in particular ways. We all have a preferred learning style, acknowledging that learning styles' inventories and questionnaires are a rather blunt tool in thinking about our own learning processes. It is also important to remember that students have very different starting points, in terms of previous experiences, both personal and professional as well as educational. It is imperative that practice educators consider the starting point of the student placed with them, and have clearly articulated notions of expected development over the course of the placement. Development, however, might not necessarily be linear. What is also important in this complicated debate is to consider the difference between so-called 'normal' and temporary blocks to learning and development, and something more concerning, that *might* be indicative that there is a *potential* that the student *may* not reach the required standards. This first section therefore deals with so called 'normal' blocks or challenges that are found in all placement learning situations.

Temporary blocks to learning

It could reasonably be expected that any student about to start placement (like any of us starting a new job) would be experiencing a range of sentiments, including trepidation, apprehension and nervousness as well as more positive emotional states such as excitement. Students may feel daunted and may experience feelings of self-doubt. For example, they may be concerned about whether they are 'good enough' to become qualified practitioners. Some students may need to 'unlearn' as well as build on their previous experiences, both personal and professional. Students may also forget that they already have skills and knowledge to develop further. At times, however, such anxieties, may have an adverse impact on their progress and development, and there may be unconscious resistance to learning and/or indeed, 'unlearning'. There is a need therefore for the learning team around the student to recognise and discuss this with the student. This does not mean, however, that the student is 'failing'. The following case vignette encourages further thought about this.

Case vignette 1

May is a student on a BA (Hons) Social Work course. She is 45 years old and of White British origin. She previously worked for over 15 years as an unqualified youth justice worker in a neighbouring local authority. Her previous placement was in a voluntary agency that supported migrants without recourse to public funds. May is on her final placement in a statutory initial assessment team for children and families. It is now week five and May has three cases assigned to her. One of the cases has a youth offending element but the focus of the social services intervention concerns allegations of domestic abuse by the stepfather towards the mother. May appears focused on the youth offending element (one of the children in the family is known to the youth offending team) and is highly critical of the youth offending worker. You feel that May is not sufficiently focused on the reason for the referral – that is, the allegation of domestic abuse – evidenced by May's home visit to the family, during which only issues around the son's youth offending were explored. You also notice that the other two cases assigned to May have not 'taken off' in a way you would expect.

Reflective exercise 2.1: What do I do?

- Why do you think May has focused on the 'wrong' issue?
- What might May be feeling right now?
- What would your feelings be at this point?
- What would you do to help May refocus? List your strategies.
- What would your strategies be in relation to the other cases where work does not seem to be progressing?
- On a scale of 1 to 10 (1 being no concerns, 10 being very concerned), how would you rate this situation in terms of whether May is a potentially failing student?

We could accurately hypothesise that May is a very experienced youth justice worker but has not yet understood the role of a social worker in a statutory children and families team. It would be understandable that she has focused on what she knows. There is a supportive conversation to be had therefore about how it can feel to be in a completely different placement, in a new local authority with a new role and remit. Acknowledging the challenges of 'unlearning' and 'relearning' may also be a helpful way forward in this scenario. Now consider the following vignette.

Case vignette 2

It is now week 10 of May's placement. You honestly feel that May presents as a bit of a 'know it all' and you are rightfully concerned that this is a very judgemental position for you to hold. There has been some progress on May's three cases to date, but you feel reluctant to allocate further cases. In supervision, your assessment is that attempts to get May to reflect more deeply on the cases rather than focus on case management and surface process have been met with defensiveness. You feel that May does not appreciate the importance of reflective practice. May repeatedly responds that she had in effect been doing social work practice in her previous role for 15 years and just needs the social work qualification in order to ensure that she is paid appropriately and can progress. May is very clear that she intends to go back into youth offending work when she graduates.

Reflective exercise 2.2: What do I need to do now?

- What would your feelings be at this point (be honest)?
- What might May be feeling right now?
- What do you think might be some of the underlying causes of May's current approach?
- Why might you be reluctant to give May more cases?
- Would you address the situation of May's motivations for becoming a social worker? If yes, why/if no, why?
- How would you encourage May to appreciate the importance of reflective practice?
- On a scale of 1 to 10 (1 being no concerns, 10 being very concerned), how would you rate this situation in terms of whether May is at risk of not meeting the requirements?

Do you now have a different level of concern? What might your feelings tell you about the situation? Is this a student at risk of failing the placement?

How do we know if a student is at risk of failing?

One possible approach is to consider more generally the behaviours or attitudinal perspectives that may be indicative that a student is struggling, or potentially at risk of failing the placement. Indeed, this has been an approach taken in previous research, and is one that I refer to as the 'trait' approach (Finch, 2010). An early but still relevant study by Brandon and Davies (1979) focused on areas where students might be failing:

- activity with clients and others in the client's environment;
- attitudes and values expressed through work;
- ability to communicate with the agency;
- communication through reports, letters, files and process records;
- availability and application of relevant theory;
- student as a learner including use of supervision;
- professional presentation;
- general conduct and behaviour at the placement. (1979, p 315)

If we relate this back to the case vignette, we could reasonably conclude that May does not yet seem to be able to use supervision effectively. Of course, this feels very broad and ill-defined at the moment, as it does not tell us what specific behaviours students (or May) will possibly engage in, or the characteristics the student may display that cause concern. Syson with Baginsky (1981) in a general study looking at placements cite the following as indicators of a student at risk of failure:

- inability to learn or develop;
- inability to apply theory to practice;
- personality/personal problems;
- rigidity. (1981, p 144)

Using a similar strategy, Williamson et al (1985) suggested that grounds for failure would include personality factors and weakness in, and application of, knowledge and skills, which included poor assessment skills, failure to meet deadlines and inadequate communication (1985, p 27). Fisher (1990) identified 21 characteristics and behaviours that may indicate a potentially failing student, including 'tactless', 'aggressive' and 'works with mouth rather than with ears' (1990, p 20). Duffy (2003), in her research on British nursing mentors, found that indicators of a weak student included '... lack of practical skills, poor communication, lack of interpersonal skills ... [and] lack of interest and absence of professional boundaries' (Duffy, 2003, p 29).

Schaub and Dalrymple (2011), in their study of British practice educators, found that concerns about students at risk of failing centred on poor or inappropriate communication, lack of professionalism, lack of adherence to social work values and lack of insight. If we applied the criteria, traits or behaviours suggested here to May, would this affect how you would assess your level of concern?

Reflective exercise 2.3: Failing student traits

- Devise a list of traits, characteristics and behaviours that may be indicative of a student at risk of not meeting placement requirements.
- What strategies have you used/will you use if you encounter these?
- What are the signs and indications that might be difficult to evidence, prove or address
- What might be the limitations of the 'trait approach'?

In 2015, practice educators at a training event in Scotland on working positively with struggling or failing students in practice learning settings were set the task of devising a list of traits and behaviours, and came up with the following suggestions:

- avoidance;
- struggling with reflection;
- cannot analyse situations;
- cannot see complexity in situations or scenarios;
- dishonest;
- value base a concern;
- student blames other for own mistakes;
- not doing a reflective diary or refusing to share;
- lack of confidence;
- lack of boundaries;
- lack of professionalism;
- not motivated or enthusiastic;
- personal factors getting in way;
- always off sick;
- social working the student;
- invading personal space and boundaries;
- not following clear and direct instructions;
- not preparing adequately;
- poor time keeping;
- overtalking (not listening);
- not producing work;

- too needy;
- cannot relate theory to practice;
- avoiding supervision. (Finch, 2015)

It is important to note our emotional response when we read through this list. Consider the following questions:

Reflective exercise 2.4: Failing traits

- Are these 'traits' similar or different from those on your list?
- Are the traits clear-cut or subjective?
- Do some of the suggestions feel judgemental and oppressive?
- If so, which ones feel problematic?

In my doctoral research (Finch, 2010) I noted the ability of practice educators to readily engage in a similar exercise. They were able to identify hypothetically what might cause a student to fail a placement, but when asked to narrate a story of their experience of working with a struggling or failing student some appeared unable to recognise those failing traits, previously identified, in the behaviour and conduct of the student.

This perhaps suggests that knowing the so-called 'signs and symptoms' does not necessarily mean that practice educators will recognise or effectively manage these concerns. This perhaps feels similar to social work more generally, where training on, or knowledge of signs and symptoms of, a range of issues only has limited effectiveness, and social workers fail to 'see' what in hindsight are obvious symptoms of, for example, child abuse. A useful article by Cooper (2005) documents this 'unseeing' in relation to Victoria Climbié, a child killed by her adopted aunt. Why practice educators can sometimes fail to see, or indeed, fail to address issues of concern is a key theme running through this book.

Limitations of the trait approach

Clearly there are limitations to the trait approach. The subjective nature of some of the traits can be somewhat problematic and on their own are not sufficient grounds for failure. As suggested earlier, practice educators may not always recognise the signs and symptoms indicating that a student is struggling. The other consideration is that students are expected to make mistakes, and of course it is the learning from these mistakes, and attitude towards them, that is the more important and decisive factor. The crucial task for practice educators is not only to be cognisant of indicators that all may not be well, but to then respond appropriately.

There is also a significant danger that if a student becomes labelled as 'failing', all subsequent behaviour may be seen as evidence of 'failing' rather than 'normal' learning and development (Goodman, 2004). We could also usefully hypothesise that a student labelled as failing may be understandably reluctant to ask for help and support, in case this is viewed as further evidence of failing. A more user-friendly and considerate approach to the question of how we might identify a student at risk of failing a placement is explored by Williams and Rutter (2015). They combine the most positive elements of the trait approach, while considering areas of concern that are not compatible with good enough social work practice. As such, Williams and Rutter (2015) identify the following:

- failure to fully engage with the learning process;
- personal or health issues that reduce a student's capacity to fully engage with or complete tasks;
- lack of confidence that affects autonomous practice, safe decision making and resilience;
- lack of the necessary critical reflection, analysis and self-awareness;
- lack of professionalism, which may include poor time keeping and a failure to follow procedures;

- issues with values, for example not recognising the impact of one's personal values on practice;
- issues with learning or assessment, for example not providing evidence of capability at the appropriate standard and not making the expected progress.

If we use this checklist to consider the case vignette, we could make a reasonably objective assessment that there is a need for May to develop in two key areas, first in how she engages in the learning process, and second in terms of demonstrating critical reflection, analysis and self-awareness. Note how this has been phrased, as areas for development rather than evidence of possible failing. It is also useful to consider what the student is neglecting to do, for example not using supervision effectively, not turning up on time or not identifying risk factors in a given scenario, or what the student *is* doing, but not doing appropriately, effectively or safely. Such a distinction can aid first with identifying clearly and explicitly those areas of development that are needed, second with writing a clear action plan detailing what needs to change, and third with ensuring that teaching strategies are in place to support the student. We explore this further in Chapter Four.

What is it to 'fail' the placement?

This is not a straightforward question to answer, which adds further to the complexities and ambiguities of practice learning more generally. For example, if there is a competency or capability assessment framework in place, and if a student can meet the required standard in some of those areas but not all, does this mean they have failed the placement? The simple answer may be yes, as they have not reached the required standard in all the required areas. There may be a related question about how far achievement in other areas mitigates or 'outweighs' the areas not fully evidenced or met? Another issue may relate to a student who has made some development after concerns have been noted but perhaps not enough. Of course, how much is enough, if students all have different starting points? A further thorny issue that can sometimes emerge concerns students who are technically competent yet cannot sufficiently relate what they are doing to theoretical frameworks. What about students whose value base is of concern, yet appear to be saying the 'right things'? Another issue again might concern students who can do the practical aspects of the job, but cannot write to agency standards. Are all these circumstances evidence of student failure?

An additional complicating factor in this debate is that different universities in the UK have different assessment regulations. Within social work education, it is common practice for the placement to be constructed as a distinct, credit-bearing module (or if not credit-bearing, at least has to be passed). Many universities allow students two attempts to pass each module. If the placement module is treated like any other academic module (and this is where universities may have different approaches), in theory the student has the 'right' to make a further attempt at passing the placement, which suggests that unless suitability issues have been identified all students have an automatic right to undertake a further placement. In some universities, including my own, there are a number of outcomes available. If a student has passed the placement but the written requirements to support the placement (usually a portfolio and sometimes a case study essay) have not met the requirements, they will be allowed a further opportunity to resubmit their portfolio or written assignment based on the placement they have just undertaken. Another option, should a practice educator have recommended a fail in terms of the placement, would be to consider the mitigating circumstances of that failed placement. This might include factors relating to the placement itself – perhaps the learning opportunities were not appropriate or the support available to the student not sufficient – or to the student, for example health or personal issues that have had a negative impact. If the student is able to take full responsibility for the concerns about their practice and has clear strategies for a positive way forward, a further placement could be offered. Another option would be that, given the extent of the concerns raised during the placement and a lack of student insight into the issues raised, a further placement would not be offered, effectively meaning that the student would be unable to complete the course and would be exited from the social work programme at that point – meaning they have effectively failed the course.

Failing placements and practice educators?

Research in the UK has highlighted that certain groups are at greater risk of failing social work training than others. Hussein et al (2008, 2009) and Moriarty et al (2009) found that female students of Black African origin, students with disabilities and men were at greater risk of failure than other groups. Furthermore, progression for black and minority ethnic groups was slower in comparison with other groups, due to retaking modules or periods of intermission. Two studies, one undertaken in Scotland (Hillen, 2013) and one in England (Fairtlough et al, 2014), had similar findings, namely that black and minority ethnic students took longer to complete their course, and were overrepresented in fails, particularly in placement fails. Students with disabilities and gay, lesbian, bisexual and transgender students were also found to have slower progression on social work programmes and were disproportionately represented in fail situations.

Schaub (2015) argues that men are the group most likely to withdraw from or fail a social work programme, although he does not distinguish if there are differences between undergraduate or postgraduate students, nor focus on any correlation between ethnicity and men. The question that has to be asked therefore is whether there are disproportionate numbers of black men failing compared with their white male peers.

In terms of practice education in the UK, Tedam (2014b) highlights some extremely disturbing incidents of racism perpetrated by white practice educators on students of Black African origin. One example concerned a white practice educator who put the phone down on a student, claiming not to understand the student's accent. A study by Zuchowski et al (2013) in Australia focused on the experiences of Aboriginal and Strait Islander social work students on placements and found that many students experienced distressing levels of racism.

The issue of ethnicity and race also emerged in Finch's (2010) study of practice educators. Both white and black practice educators felt particularly guilty when they failed black students, and white practice educators in particular questioned how far their assessments were fair and bias-free. One practice educator commented that she had only failed students of African origin in her career to date, and that caused her great consternation, and that she needed to think about whether the reasons for failing these students were influenced by her own unconscious prejudice and racism, as well as structural discrimination and oppression inherent in university assessment regimes that are based on particular western norms and practices. Thinking about structural oppression and giving honest consideration to our inherent power or powerlessness is key in addressing discrimination and prejudice, as well as a basic requirement for practice educators, as explored in Chapter Five.

It is clear therefore that placements and practice educators may let down students by failing to offer appropriate learning opportunities, having inappropriate expectations about a student – in terms of what they ought to know or have had experience of, or expecting the student to undertake work far beyond their competence – or indeed abusing the power of the practice educator role by not adhering to social work values or, as the research disturbingly shows, engaging in racist or oppressive practices.

Learning check

- What are three key issues I have learnt from this chapter?
- What are three key changes I will make in my practice, in terms of how I engage with the consideration of appropriate student development over the course of the placement?
- How will I further develop my anti-oppressive practice education?

Chapter summary

As this chapter has demonstrated, what is good enough social work is a contested concept, as social work looks different in different agencies, and is practised in many different ways. Relating this to the contested task of practice education, not least the multifaceted role, and what is good enough to pass a placement is equally complicated. Yet despite the various assessment frameworks in place to support this process, this does not appear to make the task any more straightforward. While there are limitations and difficulties in utilising the trait approach, an awareness of the signs and symptoms that may be indicative of the struggling student is nonetheless important. The chapter has also noted the issues around the relatively slower progression and disproportionate fails in certain student groups, which highlights ongoing structural oppression and discrimination as well as individual racist practices that serve only to let down both students and the profession.

Further reading

Bartoli, A., Kennedy, S. and Tedam, P. (2008) 'Practice learning: who is failing to adjust? Black African student experience of practice learning in a social work setting', *Journal of Practice Teaching and Learning*, vol 8, no 2, pp 75-90.

Bernard, C., Fairtlough, A., Fletcher, J. and Ahmet, A. (2014) 'A qualitative study of marginalised social work students' views of social work education and learning', *British Journal of Social Work*, vol 44, pp 1934-49.

Brandon, J. and Davies, M. (1979) 'The limits of competence in social work: the assessment of marginal students in social work education', *British Journal of Social Work*, vol 9, no 3, pp 295-347.

THE EMOTIONAL IMPACT OF WORKING WITH A STRUGGLING STUDENT

"I think that it's an extremely emotional, gut-wrenching kind of experience [failing a student in practice]….I don't think it feels good on any level." (Gizara and Forrest, 2004, p 136)

Introduction

This chapter considers the emotional impact, and the subsequent consequences, that may arise when working with a student who is struggling or at risk of failing a placement. The chapter begins by asking readers to engage in a series of reflective exercises that focus on motivations for becoming a practice educator, and to consider their own educational experiences, and personal and familiar attitudes towards learning. Readers are also invited to consider previous experiences of failing, as this is the first step towards successfully working with and helping students develop. The chapter goes on to document research studies that highlight the range of strong, uncomfortable and difficult emotional responses that may emerge when practice educators are confronted with a struggling or potentially failing student. The emotional processes at play will be explored using a range of theories, notably transactional analysis, Karpman's drama triangle and projective identification. Overall, the chapter seeks to encourage engagement and reflection on the emotional environment that is inherent in all practice teaching relationships and understand the emotional dynamics that come to the fore when a student is struggling in the placement.

Failing

The word 'failing' is emotive, and is often imbued with deep negativity. All of us will have experienced 'failure'; we will have failed at something in our lives, or indeed have been failed by something or someone. A starting point is to consider our thoughts and feelings about working with a potentially struggling or failing student.

Reflective exercise 3.1: Initial feelings

- How would you feel about working with a student who might struggle or go on to fail a placement?
- What do you think would be the challenges in working with a struggling student?
- Would you consider taking on a student who had previously failed a placement?

It is important to acknowledge any anxieties that arise when considering your responses to these questions. An honest response to the first question may be that practice educators would prefer not to work with a struggling student and this may be for a variety of reasons, from not wanting to fail someone to being concerned about the amount of work it might entail. Some of us may also prefer to avoid the emotional pain of failing a student. The chapter now moves on to a series of reflective exercises, beginning with an exploration of the motivations for becoming a practice educator.

Why am I a practice educator?

There are many reasons why people are motivated to become practice educators. Most of these reasons are altruistic, perhaps wanting to give something back to the profession, ensuring the maintenance of high standards within the profession or ensuring a constant supply of newly qualified professionals. These might better be described as intrinsic motivations and rewards. There may also be extrinsic reasons, both positive and negative, for becoming a practice educator, such as having had a really good practice educator as a student and wanting to emulate them, or the converse – having had a poor experience of a practice educator as a student, and not wanting another student to have to go through that negative experience. In some professions, of course, there may be a compulsion to become a practice educator to ensure career progression. In the UK, some social work practice educators are paid directly by their local authorities or agencies, which may be a factor in agreeing to work with a student. In Canada, Globerman and Bogo (2000) noted a trend for social work field instructors to be motivated more by extrinsic reasons than intrinsic ones. Nonetheless, they identified the following as key motivations for taking on the role: working in an organisation that appeared to value 'learning'; the positive contribution made by the student in the agency; and the personal growth and development as a social worker inherent in acting as a field instructor. Likewise, Schaub and Dalrymple's (2011) study found that motivations included a desire to see students grow and develop into confident practitioners; a belief in the necessity to train future generations of social workers; the positive impact the role had in refreshing social worker practitioners' knowledge of theory; and the opportunity it provided for critical reflection on social workers' own practice.

Whatever the reasons, it is important nonetheless to critically reflect on your motivation for undertaking the practice educator role. This may reveal something about your approach to the task and the subsequent attitudes or feelings you develop towards the student, as well as providing an opportunity to critically consider how far your own needs, assumptions and motivations impact on a teaching and learning relationship. It may also be very useful, in the early stages of a placement, to make your motivations, both intrinsic and extrinsic, explicit to the student. This would begin a conversation about the student's motivation for entering the profession and act as a starting point for modelling critically reflective and self-aware practice.

Reflective exercise 3.2: Attitude towards practice learning

- What were my own experiences of practice educators when I was a student?
- What did they do well?
- What could they have improved upon?
- What are my intrinsic motivations for taking on the practice educator role?
- What are my extrinsic motivations for taking on the practice educator role?

Thinking critically about motivations for taking on the role of practice educator is always important, but is even more necessary when students present with challenges or difficulties on placement. This is because students:

- may not appreciate the amount of work and thought that goes into setting up and managing a placement and the work that goes into supporting and assessing a student;
- may critically question your motivation and practice;
- may not fully appreciate your ultimate gatekeeping role and responsibilities to service users;
- may not show you the 'gratitude' you may think you 'deserve'.

Of course, these are emotive and somewhat controversial statements, but such feelings can arise all too readily in teaching and learning relationships. Keeping in mind your motivations, both intrinsic and extrinsic, will help temper such negative thoughts, which, given their unpalatability, may often be denied.

A key theme running throughout this book is recognising and working positively with the emotional dynamics at play in teaching and learning relationships. As part of this, reflecting on our formative educational experiences is also important, as our attitude towards learning, and therefore teaching, can be shaped unconsciously by previous educational experiences, as well as previous relationships with authority figures (Hunt and West, 2006). The use of psychodynamic theory to make sense of the complex world of practice education is recommended, albeit that psychodynamic theory, particularly in social work, has somewhat fallen out of favour (Bower, 2005). There are well-founded concerns about such theories, namely that they can be experienced as oppressive and pathologising, in that some of the contributions are potentially sexist or homophobic (Cosis-Brown, 1998; Payne, 2005). Furthermore, these theories may individualise problems or fail to take adequate account of the impact of environmental or structural factors in human functioning. Another criticism is that they lack measurable outcomes (Cosis-Brown, 1998). As Ruch (2000) argues, however, an integrated model of learning needs to take account of both personal and professional experience, where both impact on each other in a dynamic and fluid way. Therefore paying attention to both internal and external worlds is important for successful and confident practice education. I would argue that psychodynamic theory is the most relevant theory when trying to make sense of emotions, and can be useful for illuminating our thinking about internal worlds, particularly when exploring the issues of struggling or failing students. A major contribution of psychodynamic theory therefore is to connect our past experiences to the present day, to enable reflection on the responses, attitudes and feelings that arise in teaching and learning situations.

Psychodynamic theory

In brief, psychodynamic theory, has, as its most basic tenet, the contention that our early childhood experiences directly affect our adult functioning, and, central to this perspective, is the importance of the unconscious in human functioning (Brearly, 1991; Bower, 2005). Within social work, a useful definition of the psychodynamic approach is the focus on relationships between 'self and significant people, past and present experience, inner and outer reality' (Brearly, 1991, pp 49-50). A psychodynamic approach aims at encouraging people to reflect on, and engage with, their thought processes and feelings (Hunt and West, 2006). I would argue that this is a core aspect of practice education, namely facilitating a student to reflect both on the work undertaken and what it evokes for them personally and professionally.

Psychodynamic theory is relevant and illuminating in terms of practice education in considering the emotions at play in teaching and learning relationships. This is because, as discussed earlier, such theories also make the connection between our early childhood experiences with our primary attachment figure, and subsequently the connection with our early experiences in educational settings. These are accordingly influential in how adults respond in learning and teaching situations (Salzberger-Wittenberg et al, 1983; Coren, 1997; Hunt and West, 2006; Youell, 2006). To that end, practice educators need to think about these matters and also encourage students to do so.

Early experiences of education

Salzberger-Wittenberg et al (1983) argue that being in an adult learning environment may provoke unconscious thoughts and feelings that emanate from our early experiences of significant adults, namely our primary attachment figure. This, in turn, may affect how we experience and respond to later educational experiences. It is useful at this point to consider both our early experiences of education as well as familial attitudes towards education.

Reflective exercise 3.3: Formative experiences of education

- What is your earliest memory of being in nursery or school?
- Is it a good, bad or indifferent memory?
- Recall three strong memories you have about your primary and secondary education.
- Are they positive, negative or indifferent memories?
- What are the feelings that are raised when thinking about these memories?
- Who was your favourite teacher? Why?
- Who was your worst teacher? Why?
- Were you labelled at school (for example, the clever one, the naughty one)?
- If so, how did that label make you feel?
- Does this label still affect your sense of self as a learner?

It is worth reflecting how comfortable you felt undertaking this exercise. The following exercise asks you to reflect on your continuing journey through higher education and to consider familial and cultural attitudes towards learning.

Reflective exercise 3.4: Attitudes towards learning

Higher education	Familial attitudes
Recall three strong memories you have about your time in higher education.	Was education considered important in your family when you were growing up?
Are they positive, negative or indifferent memories?	Did your family label you as a particular 'type' of learner?
What are the feelings that are raised when thinking about these memories?	Is education considered important in your wider community?
How would you define or label yourself as a 'learner'?	How did your family support you (or not) in your early and then later education?

Debrief

How did it feel to engage in these reflective exercises? Did it feel uncomfortable or exposing? Did it raise uncomfortable memories? Familial attitudes to learning are key in how students respond to you; for example, constructive criticism may raise an unconscious memory of a critical parent or teacher.

These exercises were not designed to make you feel uncomfortable, but if uncomfortable memories and feelings that emanate from them are not thought about and made conscious, the task of practice education and thinking about students' emotional responses may become further obscured. It might be useful for all students to engage in these exercises, and of course they are vital avenues to explore when a student appears to be struggling. This at least ensures that we are supporting the student fairly and transparently, trying to find out why a student may be behaving in a certain way, and offering a jointly negotiated response to overcome any blocks to learning.

Failing and feelings

It is important now to bring to mind how failing feels, so that in turn we can appreciate the range of difficult and complex feelings a student at risk of failure may be experiencing. We need to be sufficiently 'open' to hearing and feeling the student's emotional state of mind, and our task is to help the student make sense of their complex feelings. This is not an easy task, however, as the rest of the chapter demonstrates. The following reflective exercise focuses on the experience of failing.

Reflective exercise 3.5: Getting in touch with feelings of failure

On a piece of paper, write down your responses to the following questions. Use any language you like, professional or non-professional, or if you prefer, draw pictures or symbols to honestly capture what you feel.

- What have you failed at in the past?
- How did it make you feel at the time?
- How do you feel now when you think about it?

Now fold your piece of paper up, put it away somewhere safe, and come back to it later on in this chapter.

Emotional challenges

Many experiences of education are inextricably linked to either passing or failing, not least in terms of exams, essays and assignments or learning a skill such as driving that requires a 'test'. I recall vividly Friday afternoon spelling and multiplication tests at school, and the shame I felt if I did not perform as well as I had hoped. I have maintained throughout this book that failing a student can be emotionally painful and difficult and now it seems like a good time, perhaps long overdue, to consider the research literature on which this bold assertion is based.

The research across professions notes how difficult and challenging it can be to fail students. The quote at the start of this chapter aptly and starkly demonstrates how the experience of working with a struggling student can leave one feeling. Indeed, the term 'gut-wrenching' (Gizara and Forrest, 2004, p 136) brings to mind both the mental and physical pain that can emerge. The study by Gizara and Forrest explored the views of American counselling psychology supervisors who found the experience to be far from positive, and left many with uncomfortable and difficult feelings. An earlier study by Samec (1995) documented paralysing feelings of shame experienced by supervisors working with failing trainee psychotherapists.

In the UK, there have been a number of social work studies that have explored the emotional experience of working with a struggling or failing student. Schaub and Dalrymple (2011) found that practice educators' emotional responses to working with struggling and failing students included 'fear; anger; (mis)trust; compassion; relief; and irritation' (2011, p 13). The experience was described by one practice educator in their study as 'raw' (2011, p 13). The impact on both the practice educator and sometimes the team where the student was placed was also significant, with teams feeling 'helpless' as well as unsettled, and feeling threatened and persecuted by the student.

A study by Basnett and Sheffield (2010) also documented the emotional impact on practice educators who had worked with a struggling or failing student. The experience was felt as stressful, which subsequently had an adverse impact on some practice educators' physical and mental health. The study notes in particular how practice educators experienced anxiety when they struggled to make sense of the situation with the student. Some practice educators reported feeling helpless that they could not effect change in the student. For some this prompted introspection and self-blame. For example, one practice educator commented:

"… oh troubled really troubled, as a social worker what you do is you check out a problem, and I was thinking, oh it's me. With all that reflecting, I thought it was me. I was thinking, it's me, clearly me. My style isn't working…." (Basnett and Sheffield, 2010, p 2137)

A further theoretical exploration by Schaub and Dalrymple (2013) notes how isolated practice educators felt at the time, as well as a experiencing a sense of surveillance – by their students, agency and colleagues, as well as by the university – which added to their isolation and sense of burden and pressure. My doctoral study, Finch (2010), also notes the strong and complex emotional feelings experienced by practice educators in this situation. These feelings included rage, anger, guilt and sadness. Indeed, the way the feelings were expressed by some practice educators was stark and uncompromising, and detracted from a professional discourse to a concerning degree. For example, one respondent in the study, Daisy, expressed her feeling thus: "… and I did actually think the next time you shout at me [the student], I might actually shout back at you because who the fuck do you think you are …" (Finch, 2010, p 89).

Practice educators expressed anger at the university, as well as the individual student. Alongside the anger, there was guilt. Daisy, full of rage one moment, was full of guilt the next, when recounting her story of a failing student. She comments: "Oh my God! She's been on this course a couple of years, the sacrifices she's made, I've been there myself, this is her livelihood, her career and it's all my fault …" (Finch, 2010, p 103).

As in the previous studies explored, some practice educators reported psychosomatic symptoms as well as stress. For example, Clare commented that "it was the first fail, I felt terribly guilty, I felt really … I had sleepless nights, felt quite sick, I felt incredibly guilty …' (Finch, 2010, p 104).

Practice educators, and sometimes teams, also experienced intense helplessness and despair when they could not help the student develop and learn. Tim, for example, commented: "I think the team just felt helpless in a way. They felt … they couldn't see what they could do to turn it around" (Finch, unpublished quote from 2010 research).

Alongside the guilt and feelings of helplessness, practice educators reported feeling that they had failed. For example, one research participant commented: "I actually felt it was my failing because I wasn't getting it [evidence] out of her….' (Finch, 2010, p 106). And

Terry, in a similar vein, commented that: "That was the issue I was struggling with through this whole thing. How much of her failure [the student's] was my fault?" (Finch, 2010, p 107).

These intense emotional feelings and dynamics are not just a UK social work phenomenon. Canadian social work academics Bogo et al (2007) found that field educators experienced a 'value conflict' when having to make decisions to fail students on placement. This was because the values of the profession – namely a commitment to respecting diversity, to valuing and promoting strengths, empowerment and advocacy, to facilitating growth and to developing positive relationships – were felt to be in direct conflict with the gatekeeping role whereby field instructors were required to adhere to normative standards of professional behaviour and conduct, and fail a student who was not able to meet the required standards. Field educators starkly experienced this tension as a deeply disturbing and troubling contradiction, one that caused stress and anxiety.

The emotional pain that may arise when working with a struggling student is also seen in the nursing literature. For example, Duffy's (2003) study of nursing mentors found that failing a student was emotionally stressful. Like the Canadian social work study discussed earlier, nurse mentors felt a contradiction in their role as 'caring nurses' (Duffy, 2003, p 80) when having to fail a student. Nurse mentors in the study reported feeling exhausted, sad and angry. They also reported feeling undermined and often under attack from the students.

Indeed, a sense of being persecuted by the students was also reported in Finch and Schaub, (2015). One of the practice educators, Lily, powerfully represented this feeling of being 'under attack' in the following excerpt: "she [student] put the fear of God into me … she beat me down really with threats and I allowed myself to be beaten down" (Finch and Schaub, 2015, p 309).

Another practice educator in the same study commented:

"I explained again, that I was going to fail him, and he became sort of aggressive, you know the silent sort of aggression?

Intimidating like, you know, what are you doing failing me? It was very unpleasant in his reaction to me." (2015, p 309)

As some of these studies document, the emotional drama that unfolds can be intense. This leads us to consider first, the possible consequences of such intense emotionality on the assessment process itself, and second, the underlying psychological processes that may account for such intense emotional responses and the subsequent impact on the assessment practice.

Possible impact on the assessment process

As discussed in Chapter One, there is a concern that practice educators from a range of professions may find it difficult, or be reluctant, to fail students in practice learning settings. A failure to fail contention was mooted, although there is limited empirical evidence to support this contention. We can only say very speculatively that there *may* be *some* evidence of a failure to fail by *some* practice educators, but, as Chapter Five documents, there is also *some* evidence that *some* practice educators are failing students when required, and carry out this task without experiencing paralysing levels of emotionality.

To what extent do high levels of distress affect the assessment process? Duffy (2003) found that they did have an impact, with mentors not always failing students when required. Finch et al's (2013, p 10) study highlighted some examples of students who, with hindsight, should have been failed. Indeed, one practice educator in the study commented that passing a particular student "… has been one of the worst career decisions I have ever made, and to this day, I still have a huge regret".

Finch et al (2013) argued that one of the consequences of such emotionality was that it had a negative impact on practice educators' reflective capabilities, which subsequently got in the way of timely interventions and a carefully considered assessment report. This in turn may have prevented practice educators' recommendations from being upheld by the subsequent university panels. Finch et al (2013) continue with this theme of the possible impact of high levels of distress to argue that the consequences of uncontained emotionality led to poor relations with the university, blame and splitting – into categories of 'good' or 'bad' student, and 'good' or 'bad' tutor – and abruptly ended placements that did not always follow university placement termination procedures. Let us now return to the last reflective exercise.

Getting in touch with feelings of failure

Reflective exercise 3.5 asked you to reflect on a failing experience and recall how it made you feel, both at the time and subsequently. The reflective 'failure' exercise is a powerful way of thinking deeply and personally about the impact of failing something, or of being failed. This is useful for a number of reasons. First, it reminds us how deeply painful failing is and how it can stay with us, often in an unconscious way. Second, it helps us to think deeply about students' feelings about the possibility of failure. Third, from a psychodynamic perspective, the student is likely to project these difficult feelings on to the practice educator, as they may be too uncontaining and difficult for the students themselves to acknowledge, process and hold. Perhaps they have had previous experiences of failure in their lives, which are unconsciously evoked by the current situation. As such, if practice educators can view these projections as a form of communication rather than internalising them, it may well be helpful to describe the feelings back to the student.

In the spirit of not asking anyone to do anything I would not do myself, I recall an incident of my own failure, namely being unable to get an article on failing students accepted for publication. The feedback from the anonymous reviewers was, in hindsight, very helpful, but at the time I remember feeling angry and hostile towards the reviewers. I just could not understand what was required of me, and I had a strong physical reaction, a horrible feeling of dread in my stomach, when reading the feedback. I felt stupid and inadequate and I recall feeling quite tearful. I had a strong sense of 'rejection', although as someone wise pointed out, the paper had not been rejected, rather it needed major revision. Yet the feeling of rejection, hurt and inadequacy was very strong indeed, and I felt like that child again who had not done well enough in the weekly school spelling test.

In the end, things turned out well for the article; my former doctoral supervisor became a joint author, the paper was published (and indeed is referred to in this book) and I slowly realised what a helpful experience it had been, as I had learnt what was required in terms of writing a journal article. I also felt guilty for thinking hostile thoughts about the reviewers, who had in fact offered helpful, generous and constructive feedback. It is interesting to note that despite immersing myself in the experience of failing students, I perhaps had to go through my own 'failing academic experience' to really understand the students' position, and in turn, the impact on the practice educator. Of course, not all of these failing incidences are resolved and have a happy ending; some may well linger on, and there may not be immediate or indeed any learning derived from them.

Having carried out reflective exercises on failing with lots of practice educators over the past few years, I have discovered that their experiences often centre around failed exams at school, particularly in mathematics, failed social work placements, failed driving tests and failed relationships, with children, friends and partners. The exercises were carried out anonymously and the feelings revealed were often stark and uncompromising. The emotional responses aroused by these failing incidences often included:

- embarrassment;
- stupidity;
- shame;
- anger;
- sadness;
- hopelessness;
- confusion;
- feeling drained;
- depression;
- rage;

- unfairness;
- indignation ('I don't deserve it');
- blamelessness ('it's not my fault');
- guilt (for letting others down);
- persecution.

As can be seen, these are very powerful emotions and it was important to note that practice educators felt not just one but many emotions. For some practice educators, the events turned out well and there was a resolution – exams and placements were repeated and passed, and new relationships were found – but others still experienced regret, sadness and anger about the particular incident.

Keeping in mind the reflective exercise on failings and feelings, let us consider the following questions.

Reflective exercise 3.6: Making links to the research

- Was it uncomfortable engaging in the reflective exercise? If so, why?
- Do you notice any similarities between the feelings expressed in the research and your own feelings?
- Do you notice any differences between the feelings expressed in the research and your own feelings?
- Have you experienced these difficult feelings in your work as a practice educator?
- How did you respond to or manage these feeling in the practice learning situation?
- Any thoughts or further reflections?

Box 3.1 compares the feelings invoked by practice educators' own failing incidents (from the author's reflexive exercises with practice educators described earlier) and practice educators' emotional responses to working with a struggling or failing student, as reported in the research literature documented earlier in the chapter.

Box 3.1: Comparison of practice educators' emotional responses to their own and their students' experiences of failing

Practice educators' responses to own experiences of failing

Embarrassment	Shame
Stupidity	Anger
Sadness	Hopeless
Confusion	Drained
Depressed	Rage
Not fair	Don't deserve
Not my fault	Guilt
Persecuted	

Practice educators' responses when working with a struggling student

Anger	Rage
Isolation	Sadness
Hopeless	Despair
Guilt	Confusion
Must be my fault?	Isolation
Anxiety	Dread
Persecuted	Shame

Note where the feelings are similar and where they differ in these lists (and in your own list of feelings). What is key, however, and of far greater importance than lamenting practice educators' and indeed universities' alleged 'failure to fail', is the need to understand more fully the psychological and emotional processes behind the challenges in working with struggling or failing students. Making these processes explicit will aid practice educators considerably in understanding the emotional climate in learning situations and working more effectively and confidently as a result.

Emotional processes and models

It has been established that the emotional impact on practice educators of working with a struggling student can be significant, and may have an adverse impact on the assessment process. What is required are theories to help us understand this phenomenon, so we can remain perceptive to the unfolding dynamics between ourselves and student practitioners. It is also clear that there is little theorisation of these psychological processes within the research literature. Three theories (transactional analysis, Karpman's drama triangle and projective identification – the first two being closely linked) that may be relevant are briefly put forward here for consideration, recognising, of course, that there are a range of other theories that may be equally applicable.

Transactional analysis and Karpman's drama triangle

While transactional analysis and the drama triangle are relatively old theories that conceptualise significant interactions between people, there is some merit in relating the models to practice education. In 1968, Karpman wrote *Fairy Tales and Script Analysis*, where he proposed the idea of the 'drama triangle'. This emerged from two distinct theoretical sources – transactional analysis and family therapy, both derived from psychoanalytical ideas. A key tenet of transactional analysis is that observing dynamics between people can reveal significant issues and concerns (Berne, 1967, 1977). A further feature of this approach is the view that the human personality is made up of three ego states, each of which is a complex mass of thoughts, feelings and behaviours (Clarkson, 1992). These three ego states are known as parent, adult and child, and the interactions between the ego states is the focus of intervention (ITAA, date unknown).

Transactional analysis in its simplest form characterises interactions between people and makes explicit the point at which people fall into adult-to-child interactions and vice versa (Berne, 1977). So if an adult interacts with you in a parental way, your response is likely to be childlike. The aim, of course, is to ensure that interactions remain 'adult to adult'. This has resonance with adult learning theory, discussed in Chapter Four, and there is also a connection with the theory of learned helplessness, which contends that learning that one's actions have no influence on outcomes produces learned helplessness (Walker et al, 2004). This then affects a person's ability to master a situation by undermining cognitive and motivational functioning (Smith and Mackie, 2000). Anything that the person then perceives as a threat induces a learned helplessness response.

Karpman extended Berne's ego states idea further by arguing that in a drama triangle there exist three ego states, known as the persecutor, rescuer and victim (1977). In such a triangle, people can occupy different positions, moving from persecutor to victim, or victim to rescuer. As the research literature (and our own responses to failing) have evidenced, practice educators express feelings of both being persecuted and feeling like a victim, that is, being intimidated and feeling threatened by students. This may then affect practice educators' confidence levels and decisiveness. The rescuer mode, of course, resonates with internalising the failure as one's own, as well as the response to passive or 'helpless students'. In the context of practice education, the tutor may also adopt one of these roles or be perceived to be occupying one of those roles. Being seen as a persecutor can be quite discomforting and challenging, and of course, appears at odds with many caring professional values. This perhaps reveals why it is such an upsetting experience for practice educators to experience this value paradox, as highlighted previously in the work of Duffy (2003) and Bogo et al (2007). Again, the need for practice educators to both reflect on, and respond appropriately to, the dynamics that emerge, is vital. Recognising when our approaches and interactions are not adult to adult, or thinking about drama triangle roles, is key to confident practice education and assessment for all students.

Projective Identification

Projective identification, a theory originally proposed by Melanie Klein, is a useful and illuminating, albeit somewhat disturbing, theory, but one that can aid us nonetheless in understanding the intense and powerful emotions that can sometimes leave practice educators feeling both mentally and physically disturbed to the point that they seem to lose their reflective proficiencies and decision-making capabilities. Projective identification therefore is an unconscious defensive response, and like all unconscious defensive responses aims to protect us from real or imaginary psychological harm (Trevithick, 2011). It is conceptualised by Frosh (2012) as an unconscious communication from one person to another, but is more than transference or counter-transference (Joseph, 2012), as it evolves from the primitive projection of good and bad on to, and from, the mother, and is the projection of unpleasant parts of the self, such as urine and faeces, on to the mother or other person (Mitchell, 1991). Frosh (2012) describes this process as an 'expulsion of unwanted or threatening ideas' (p 162). A person therefore unconsciously divests themselves of the unwholesome parts that they cannot tolerate or bear, or 'are very deeply denied in the self' (Segal, 1992, p 36), and projects them on to others. In a psychotherapy setting this would be the therapist, but this could also conceivably be the practice educator (Finch et al, 2014).

Given that failing can make us feel shame, anger, rage and so on, a student at risk of failing will unconsciously project these feelings on to the practice educator. The danger of not recognising this as a projective identificatory process is that we will engage in unconscious defensive behaviours to protect ourselves from feelings that we believe may be our own (Terry, 2008). Spillius et al (2011) argue further that such unconscious projections compel the person to unconsciously act out or feel the projected behaviours, attitudes and feelings. A process of 'mobilisation' or indeed immobilisation can subsequently occur, which may result in a practitioner (or practice educator in this case) becoming confused by events and unable to thoroughly analyse what is happening. As Trevithick (2011) points out, and key to this debate, this might result in the failure 'to notice and to respond appropriately to dangerous or threatening situations' (2011, p 404), in other words failing to fail an incompetent or even dangerous practitioner.

Reflective exercise 3.7: Theories

- How do these theories relate to the research findings documented earlier?
- How do these theories apply to your own experiences of working with students in placements?
- In what ways do these theories shed any further light on your reflections about your own experiences of failing?

Learning check

- What are the three key things you have learnt from this chapter?
- What are the three key issues for you now as a practice educator?
- What are three things you might now do differently as a practice educator?

Chapter summary

This chapter has documented the intense emotional experience that may arise from working with a struggling or failing student. Acknowledging the array of complex feelings that may arise can be helpful in making sense of current or past experiences of working with struggling or failing students. It may even be helpful to some extent in normalising the challenging and disturbing feelings that may arise. These feelings are to be expected when working with a struggling student, however. The important task is to recognise the feelings rather than deny them, reflect on them and their possible causes – for example, a form of communication coming from the student, or a subconscious personal memory of a failing experience (or perhaps both these things) – and then use them productively, that is, seeing them as a form of communication rather than personal attack. It is important that we do not lose sight of our professional values, and that we work hard to understand student perspectives and maintain an appropriate degree of empathy.

Further reading

Finch, J. and Taylor, I. (2013) 'The emotional experience of assessing a struggling or failing social work student in practice learning settings, special edition – field education', *Social Work Education*, vol 32, no 2, pp 244-58, DOI: 10.1080/02615479.2012.720250.

Finch, J., Schaub, J. and Dalrymple, R. (2013) 'Projective identification and the fear of failing: making sense of practice educators' emotional experiences of failing social work students in practice learning settings', *Journal of Social Work Practice*, vol 28, no 2, pp 139-54.

Salzberger-Wittenberg, I., Williams, G. and Osborne, E. (1983) *The Emotional Experience of Learning and Teaching*, London: Karnac Books.

ASSESSMENT AND STRATEGIES FOR WORKING EFFECTIVELY WITH STRUGGLING STUDENTS

"... you can sometimes be drawn into that role, often as a rescuer ... at the same time you can be perceived as a persecutor ... I rely on my boundaries ... establishing ... you are not here to heal, you're here to learn." (Finch, 2010, p 114)

Introduction

The first step for effective practice is to reflect on one's own state of mind and consider the emotional climate. Good practice education should look the same with all students, and so the strategies detailed in this chapter should be applied to all students. The strategies, however, are particularly important for students on placement experiencing difficulties that are serious enough to indicate that the student is at potential risk of failing the placement. The chapter begins with a consideration of the role of the practice educator, with all its ambiguities and complexities. It also considers the role of the tutor, as well as the roles and responsibilities of the student. The chapter goes on to document a range of positive strategies, such as 'courageous conversations', creative approaches to the task of practice education, assessment strategies, effective use of action planning and report writing. It then considers the research evidence about why practice educators might be reluctant to fail students in practice learning settings; as knowing why something happens means we are more alert to the possibilities, namely, avoiding failing the student. The chapter then moves on to consider the strategies used by practice educators who are able to fail students without experiencing distressing levels of emotionality. Lastly, it explores issues such as the fair and transparent assessment of students and working in positive, non-discriminatory ways.

The role of the practice educator

In all practice teaching and learning situations, it is important to have a clear sense of one's role and responsibilities, as a lack of clarity leads to difficulties for everyone. Chapter One explored the numerous functions within the overall role of practice educator, and readers were asked to consider in the learning check exercise how they managed to bring together all these tasks within the overall role. An examination of the literature revealed that the notion of gatekeeper was missing from the roles discussed in the literature. Some of the research discussed in Chapter One also noted the absence of an explicit acknowledgement of the gatekeeper role for tutors as well as practice educators (Finch, 2010; Finch and Poletti, 2013; Finch, 2014). Perhaps another way of addressing this issue is to consider the distinct responsibilities of the practice educator. The practice educator is responsible for undertaking a fair and transparent assessment of the student, applying the particular assessment framework in place, and following adult learning and anti-discriminatory principles. As noted in Chapter One, there are differences in approaches in the UK, with competency models used in Northern Ireland, Wales and Scotland, and a capability approach used in England. There is a clear expectation that practice educators offer more than a supervisory function, but should enable learning opportunities as well as the learning of others.

The role of the tutor

While there may be some differences between professions, the role of the university tutor often encompasses:

- undertaking placements visits;
- ensuring that the learning opportunities offered are appropriate;
- supporting both the student and the practice educator with placement requirements and expectations;
- ensuring that the processes and policies of the university are followed.

When difficulties arise there are additional requirements, including:

- being responsive and proactive;
- not 'taking sides';
- ensuring that an action plan is developed, including clearly articulated actions for all the parties, timescales and a subsequent review.

It might well be a challenge for a tutor not to take sides, as tutors will inevitably have a view of the situation they are confronted with. Finch (2014) noted that tutors found it difficult to be in the middle of two parties, both of whom had very different views of the same situation. Certainly as a tutor, what has helped me manage wildly differing views of a situation is a clear understanding of my role, which is to ensure that universities policies and procedures are followed. This enables me comfortably to support both students and practice educators alike. I may (or may not) have a view of the situation, but it remains just that – a view. It is also important to understand that the tutor role is a powerful one, as explored further in Chapter Five, and historically played a decisive role in decision making (perhaps continuing to do so, albeit surreptitiously). As my ethnographic pilot study revealed (Finch, 2014, 2016), the social work tutor also played a powerful role in decisions about whether or not to uphold practice educators' recommendations.

The role of the student

It is important to remember that adult learning principles should be applied in all higher education situations. These are important principles to bear in mind in order to avoid getting into unhelpful dynamics, such as parent–child interactions or Karpman's (1968, 1971) drama triangle involving persecutor, victim and rescuer roles, which, as discussed in Chapter Four, may get in the way of appropriate assessment. Knowles (1970), and later Knowles et al (2015), argued that adult learning approaches need to be 'andragogical' as opposed to pedagogical, the latter being applicable for children. The andragogical approach is premised on a set of assumptions about adult learners, namely that adult learners have a range of previous experiences to draw on, are willing and able to learn and as such are largely self-directed in their learning. As explored in Chapter Four, being in an adult learning situation may provoke childhood memories of learning, resulting in unhelpful learning behaviour. It is reasonable to expect students of all professions to take a proactive approach to their learning on placements. They should not be passive recipients of practice educators' wisdom, but should be enquiring, self-directive and committed to developing their skills, knowledge and practice. Moreover, it is for the student to take the lead in evidencing how they meet the practice requirements, with the practice educator's support. The case study in Chapter Two highlighted a situation where the student struggled to engage in the learning processes in an appropriate way.

Ensuring that the roles and responsibilities of all stakeholders are clearly understood is important in all learning situations, but becomes even more necessary when there are difficulties on placements. Overprotecting a student is as damaging as not supporting a student effectively, or at all.

'Saying it as it is' or having courageous conversations

As documented in Chapter Two, the first step in the process of having a courageous conversation is identifying the difference between a normal, temporary block to learning and something more long-term and concerning. The first strategy therefore may seem obvious, namely letting the student know about an area of development they need to address. The term 'saying it as it is' is rather colloquial and on one level feels inappropriate for social work and practice education, as it may appear rather aggressive or too blunt. However, I have observed practice educators, tutors and students alike being fearful of being explicit about concerns and avoiding being overt, unambiguous and clear about contentious issues arising from a placement. As such, important information may be left 'unsaid'. 'Saying it as it is' may more appropriately be expressed as having a 'courageous conversation' (Beddoe and Davys, 2016). The authors offer a very clear and compelling account of what constitutes a courageous conversation. Such conversations have the following characteristics:

- conversations are associated with some sort of emotion;
- participants may feel ashamed, apprehensive, uncomfortable, angry and embarrassed;
- conversations may be conflicted, by introducing different ideas, values or behaviours;
- conversations may cause conflict and hurt;
- conversations may have a significant impact on relationships. (adapted from Beddoe and Davys, 2016, p 193)

Such conversations therefore are understandably often avoided and there are very real barriers to having such conversations, such as fear of hurting or offending the other person, damaging the relationship and not being able to cope with the response (Beddoe and Davys, 2016). Harvard Business Review (2016) makes the following acute observation about difficult conversations: 'You know that feeling:

that knot in the pit of your stomach; the fog descends on your mind' (2016, p 3).

The result is that sometimes such conversations are avoided, and, as Maclean (2012) comments, avoiding highlighting instances where someone is underperforming as they arise may lead to a further escalation of difficulties, whereby the problem gets worse and the situation becomes more fraught. Other reasons to avoid difficult conversations include denial of the problem at hand, a false hope that the problem will resolve itself of its own accord, or perhaps a false assumption that the person will not change anyway. This is discussed later in the chapter in the section on why practice educators might be reluctant to fail students, or why lack of timeliness in addressing an issue may arise.

Maclean's (2012) work, on social work supervision but nevertheless of huge relevance to this debate, suggests asking the following questions before having a difficult conversation with an underperforming supervisee:

- Are the expected standards set and clearly documented?
- Does the practitioner (in this case the student) understand the standards?
- In what ways are the standards not being met?
- What are the reasons for the standards not being met?

These outwardly simple questions are important considerations not only in terms of how to work effectively with struggling or failing students, but in terms of the assessment and development of all students.

Using the assessment framework well

The assessment framework is the key to understanding the extent of the developmental needs of a given student. The assessment framework clearly articulates the expected standards, recognising, of course, the subjectivities and contested nature of social work or indeed many other caring professions. At the outset, it is worth investing time in thinking about how the various learning opportunities that are available on a particular placement link to the various competences, capabilities or domains. Not only does this evidence how the placement can provide the appropriate learning opportunities, but it also helps the student think about the expected standards and how the various competences or requirements link with the work on offer.

This is not to say that assessment frameworks are without limitations or challenges, as has been intimated in other chapters. Indeed, competency approaches to the task of assessing professionals in practice have been criticised on a number of grounds (Lyons, 1999; Lymbery, 2003). O'Hagan (1996), for example, in the context of social work education, raises the following concerns about competency approaches, namely that they:

- are based on behaviourism and functional analysis, therefore they are narrow in focus, reductionist and technicist;
- are employer-led and workplace-located, and so psychologically distant from traditional academic training and therefore influenced by managerialist approaches;
- are politically motivated, aimed at reducing the power of academic institutions from which 'educational and welfare professionals emerged' (1996, p7);
- are focused on emphasising method and efficiency rather than purpose;
- reduce the importance of knowledge and values in a given profession as well as eliminating 'critical autonomy' (1996, p 13);
- are incompatible with altruism and the values of health, welfare and educational professions;
- negate the importance of multi-agency, collaborative working in favour of an individualised approach.

O'Hagan argues further that when applied to social work in particular, competency frameworks result in a tick-box approach to the task of assessment, and indeed this was borne out in research conducted by Walker et al (1995). A further criticism is that competency approaches are too simplistic to take sufficient account of the complexities and nuances of practice. O'Hagan raises particular concern about how objective competency approaches are in reality, and linked to this, how they may lack rigour in addressing issues of anti-discriminatory and anti-oppressive practice. Similarly, Kemshall (1993) has questioned how far the approach is congruent with anti-discriminatory and anti-oppressive practice values. Maclean with Lloyd (2013) argue further that such approaches focus on the assessment at the expense of learning, and in particular focus on the 'what' at the expense of 'why' and 'how' (2013, p 111).

As documented in Chapter One, what is good enough in social work is difficult to define, as are the many competencies or requirements involved. In a relatively old but important study, Owens (1995) explored how practice educators made sense of the assessment requirements in practice. The findings suggested that practice teachers showed wide variation in their interpretation of the notion of competency, and further of their understanding of minimum standards, or what Owens (1995) terms 'the bottom line' (1995, pp 67-8).

So where does that leave us, in terms of using an assessment system, with all its inherent flaws and weaknesses? There is a clear need to approach the task of assessment in a holistic way; indeed, this is the aim of the Professional Capability Framework currently used in England to assess social work students. A holistic approach attempts to move assessors and students away from the tick-box approach, where notions of competence may be in danger of being narrowly defined. A holistic approach instead takes a broader view of competence, and aims to reflect the subtleties and nuances of professional practice. So instead of a distinct competence such as communicating and engaging with people being 'ticked off' in terms of one or two examples of this happening, a holistic approach assesses this activity across the placement, seeing how it is managed in a range of situations, with a wide range of people. Assessment, therefore, is an ongoing process and takes place in a variety of ways. It is clear that social workers, whose daily tasks often involve assessment of service users, have well developed assessment skills, but these need to be reorientated to the task of learning. As Maclean with

Lloyd (2013) argue, a capability approach to the task of assessment will be centred around how and why people do things, rather than what people do, will encourage professional practice rather than focus on simplistic roles and tasks, will focus on the development of a student, rather than just meeting narrow assessment criteria, and will assess how practice is developed and analysed, rather than merely following procedure. Maclean with Lloyd (2013) make a further, really important point, namely that a practice educator should enable the student to play a central role in creating their own learning and development 'map', rather than following a pre-determined path. This links back to the point made earlier about adult learning principles.

Teaching and learning tools

For practice educators in social work, there is a clear expectation that the role is more than that of a supervisor; it is one of teacher, learning enabler and assessor. Practice educators should be developing a repertoire of teaching and learning 'tools' to aid students – in other words, creative techniques or approaches to enable students to engage fully in their learning journey. This is even more important when students experience a temporary block to learning. Some of these blocks, in my experience, often centre on two issues: applying theory to practice, and becoming more critically self-reflective and aware, that is, moving from understanding the process to developing more nuanced understandings, namely that 'what, why and how' (Maclean, 2017). In developing specific teaching tools or techniques, the underlying principle has to be one where the student is not merely being fed information, but actively participates in the activity.

Reflective exercise 4.1: Teaching tools
- List all the specific tools or techniques you utilise to enable students' learning.
- Are your tools or techniques premised on a particular approach to learning, that is, a specific learning style?
- Can you commit to utilising three approaches, techniques or learning tools to help a student apply theory to practice and promote critical (self-)reflection?

Did you find this exercise challenging? Is the term 'teaching tool' a little off-putting? Do you perhaps rely on a few tried and trusted methods? The following list of tools, which is far from exhaustive, might be useful to consider in your future work with students.

- role play – perhaps practising potentially difficult conversations;
- Johari windows (Luft and Ingham, 1955);
- the name game, where you tell the story of your name, that is, does your name have a meaning, were you named after someone, do you have other names, do you like your name?
- the use of timelines of key incidents in the student's life to explore a range of issues, for example, values, experiences of discrimination, experiences of education and so on;
- hopes and fears exercise – both practice educator and student could undertake this activity, detailing their hopes and fears for the placement; it could also be used as a way of reviewing progress;
- who am I exercise?
- learning style inventories – although do take these with a pinch of salt.

Some fantastic resources have already been developed to help you integrate a creative approach to your work. Some of the resources in *Draw on your Emotions* (Sunderland and Engleheart, 1997) are useful for helping students explore their feelings about their work, for example, or indeed thinking about resilience during their placement. Maclean's (2015a, 2015b) theory cards and reflective learning cards are both excellent resources to help you get creative in your practice. For a student who is struggling, doing something different or 'out of the box' may just be the lever required to enable the student to progress. Indeed, several years ago, a stage 2 practice educator I taught who felt very stuck in her work with a student utilised the Johari window exercise. This enabled the student to open up about some very difficult personal circumstances that were clearly affecting her ability to fully engage in the placement. The chapter now moves on to consider 'concerns' meetings and action planning.

Concerns meetings and action planning

Calling in the social work tutor and undertaking action planning is a vital part of the process when things are difficult on placement and issues cannot be resolved locally between the student and the practice educator. This process must include the social work tutor, as well as the practice educator (on- or offsite) and the on-site supervisor (if there is one). Of course, different universities may refer to these three- or four-way 'concerns' meetings in other ways, for example as disruption meetings.

The meeting is usually chaired by the tutor. It provides a forum where all parties can express their concerns, which may centre on the student, the practice educator and placement, or all three. The tutor should help both student and practice educator to be clear and non-ambiguous about the issues at stake and ask about the evidence for the views expressed. These are not always easy meetings to chair, or indeed to participate in, but this is where 'courageous conversations' are needed on the part of everyone; indeed, in social work and many other caring professions 'courageous conversations' are part and parcel of everyday work.

An action plan should come out of the concerns meeting and could cover the following areas, although readers are encouraged to adapt their plan to meet the student's needs and placement context as appropriate:

- area of concern;
- student actions and outcomes required;
- practice educator actions and outcomes required;
- date for completion;
- review date meeting.

It is important that the issues that need to be addressed are not generalised or vague, but are very clear, and linked to that, that there are clear behaviours or actions that need to be evidenced, by when and to what standard. It may be that the student fails to make the necessary development after the process has been completed, and if things slip further back after the review process, this is a clear indicator that learning cannot be sustained. The action plan should be enough to change things for the better, but if issues continue to arise, the action plan is a vital piece of evidence for the final assessment report.

Writing the assessment report

As stated earlier, good assessment reports should be the norm for all students, but there are some additional elements that are relevant for students who may not have met some of the requirements. The first obvious step is to think about one's own emotional state of mind. This is important to ensure that the assessment report you write, is fair, balanced and constructive, rather than destructive. A report should therefore:

- utilise as far as possible a wide range of objective evidence about the student's development and progress, as measured against the requirements;
- be based on a holistic assessment of the student;
- take into account the reliability and validity of judgements made;
- include the views of others, for example, service users, colleagues and so on;
- be analytical.

The student should not be surprised at the contents of the mid- or final assessment reports, as practice educators should provide the student with constant, formative feedback. If the student is unaware of any concerns, or indeed the recommendation of a fail, before they receive their report, something has gone very wrong in the process.

When recommending a fail, it may be useful to include the following in the report:

- a general overview of the key events that led up to the placement breakdown or recommendation of a fail;
- a detailed account of the learning opportunities on offer at the agency;
- what has been done to try to facilitate progress and development, which learning and teaching tools have been used, how colleagues have helped to facilitate learning, and the response to these interventions;
- an action plan and the eventual outcomes.

In a report that is recommending a fail, it is important to remain fair and balanced, and not to let frustrations or anger emerge. The student will usually have made some progress, so it is worth noting what the student has done well. Think about the language used, and draw on principles of good constructive feedback.

Such strategies and good practice guidance are all very well, but as we saw in Chapter Three, working with a struggling student remains a highly charged emotional experience. The next section of this chapter goes on to consider why it is that some practice educators may be reluctant to fail a student in a practice learning setting.

A reluctance to fail?

Chapter One briefly explored general concerns about practice learning, particularly in a social work context. One such concern was the low failure rate in social work courses, which is said to be evidence of an unwillingness to fail students. Indeed, one of the reasons for changing the social work qualification from the Certificate in Qualified Social Work to the Diploma in Social Work, as discussed in Chapter One, was a concern about the low failure rate (2-3%), which was said to be 'evidence of low standards in student selection and poor assessments that led to students passing who should not' (Sharp and Danbury, 1999, p 5). That said, the failure rate largely remained consistent even after the Diploma in Social Work was replaced by the degree in social work (Finch, 2005), and of course, on their own, failure rates tell us very little about standards in social work education.

Another concern noted in Chapter One centred on practice educators' alleged inability or reluctance to fail a student. The failure to fail contention therefore, as discussed previously, is rather contentious and there is little evidence for it; nonetheless, an international thematic review of the literature (Finch, 2013; Finch and Poletti, 2013) suggests that the following *may* be why *some* practice educators, from social work and cognate disciplines, *might* find it difficult to fail a student:

- **a failure to use the competency model of assessment appropriately or effectively** (Kemshall, 1993; Eraut, 1994; Shardlow and Doel; 1996, Furness and Gilligan, 2004; Shapton, 2006);
- **a failure to follow procedures for dealing with placement issues** (Ilott and Murphy, 1999; Burgess et al, 1998a, 1998b; Duffy, 2003; Vacha-Haase et al, 2004; Kaslow et al, 2007). This often becomes a problem in terms of addressing issues in a timely manner;
- **lack of support from practice educators' own agency or the university** (Finch, 2004a; Vacha-Haase et al, 2004; Schaub and Dalrymple, 2013). Indeed, some practice educators in Finch (2010) reported feeling that the university did not want them to fail students and felt under pressure not to do so;
- **role strain or confusion** (Fisher, 1990; Proctor, 1993; Owens, 1995; Cowburn et al, 2000; Duffy, 2003). This concerns issues previously discussed, namely the difficulty in reconciling seemingly conflictual roles;
- **fear of litigation** (Cole, 1991; Raymond, 2000; Royse, 2000; Cole and Lewis, 1993; Duffy, 2003; Vacha-Haase et al, 2004). While this stems mostly from North American contexts, it is not unknown for students to threaten legal remedies when they feel they have been unfairly treated; however it is important to note that litigation is extremely rare;

- **rule of optimism** (Vacha-Haase et al, 2004; Finch, 2005). This theory was originally developed by Dingwall et al (1983) and centres on social work practitioners' tendencies to overemphasise or overestimate the positive qualities of parents at the expense of seeing the more negative features. The same phenomenon can be seen in practice education, where the strengths demonstrated by a student may get in the way of identifying areas for development;
- **hope that things will 'sort themselves out' without intervention** (Goodman, 2004; Hoffman et al, 2005). This is also known as 'burying one's head in the sand', but as the chapter later argues, ignoring issues in the short term causes more stress and conflict in the long term.

It is worth noting your emotional reaction when reading this section, and thinking about any resonance it may have. It is also interesting to note how these issues have consistently come up in other sections of this book.

Strategies for avoiding the drama and pain

Although this subheading is rather emotive, working with a struggling student will always provoke an emotional response in the practice educator. Indeed, it would be very worrying if practice educators did not experience any emotion at the prospect of failing a student. What was so patent in my original doctoral research was the intense feelings that so starkly emerged in these situations. For some of the practice educators interviewed, I felt that some of this intense emotional drama had a negative impact on the assessment process, resulting, for example, in abruptly terminated placements (this was also seen in the research undertaken by Schaub and Dalrymple, 2011) or poorly written and evidenced assessment reports, which often led to students being given further placement opportunities when the evidence was suggestive of a clear fail. In some cases, the intense emotions experienced by all stakeholders may well have contributed to students being passed before they were ready. Indeed, one practice educator made this very honest comment:

"To be honest I kind of passed her because I was glad to get rid of her and I know that's dreadful … I feel awful … I've never forgotten her and I have a huge regret to this day … this was the worse career decision I have ever made." (Finch and Schaub, 2013, p 10)

It was striking to note in the original doctoral research (albeit that the research comprised a small-scale qualitative study, meaning that findings cannot be generalised) that a quarter of the practice educators interviewed told their stories without the drama and were in fact very reflective. I noted that this cohort appeared to find it 'easier' to go on to fail the student, whereas others appeared to have not been able to fail the student, despite at times strong evidence that the student was not fulfilling expectations or making the necessary development and progress. What was similar about the practice educators' accounts was that they:

- were explicit about their gatekeeping role and understood that this always took precedence;
- had clearly articulated boundaries around what was 'their' work and what was the students' work — hence the students' work was very much their own, and there was little use of 'we';
- had clearly articulated boundaries about their role and responsibilities towards the student, and the limits of their responsibilities towards the students;
- were able to articulate expectations about adult learners and replicate adult learning principles in their work — hence they were clear about the students' responsibilities in the learning process;
- were generally very balanced in their account of the situation, demonstrated a high level of critical reflection on the events and as such appeared at the time not to have been affected by difficult student projections;
- saw that the experience, albeit emotionally painful to some extent, provided valuable learning opportunities for their future practice.

All of this is summed up beautifully by one practice educator, who stated:

"... you know it's meant to be a mature student I am dealing with, you know, we are entering into this arrangement, right, as adults, you know I had my part to play, the student has their part to play ... I just kind of felt well, this [failing a student] is going to happen in practice placement but then, you know, as well, this is primarily your responsibility, it's your responsibility at the beginning as well, to think about what you're getting into." (Finch, 2010, p 105)

Discrimination and oppression

Practice educators have immense authority and power over a student. They are assessing the extent to which the student has met complicated practice requirements. Students inevitably feel powerless in this situation and opportunities for discrimination against students are rife. There is very limited research about the experiences of students on placement generally, and even less on the perspective of those who have failed their practice placements, with some notable exceptions such as Burgess et al (1998a, 1998b), Parker, (2010), Poletti and Anka (2013) and Tedam (2014a, 2014b). What little research there is suggests that first, the student's experience of failing a placement is always going to be incredibly painful, and second, as discussed in Chapter Two, there are a number of distinct student groups that progress more slowly, or indeed are disproportionately failed, and, as discussed earlier, there is an additional concern that competency approaches may have inherent biases within them. It is disappointing to note, therefore, that social workers training appears to be replicating, rather than challenging and subverting, structural discrimination and oppression. Maclean with Lloyd (2013) document various psychological processes that can render assessment invalid. These include the following:

- the halo or horn effect – all future behaviour is viewed through the prism of previous performance by the student;
- the 'nice' student – this may promote collusion on the part of the practice educator, who may offer more help and support to 'get them through';
- stereotyping – Tedam's (2014a, 2014b) research found that students felt certain assumptions had been made about them because of their ethnic background;
- first impressions – these may lead to the halo or horn effect;
- lack of balance – more credence is given to the negatives over the positives or vice versa (links to the law of optimism);
- inferring – making a judgements about ability in one particular area, based on capacity in another;
- similarity and difference – making a wrong judgment about a student if they go about a task differently from how the practice educator might do it (the important thing to focus on is the outcome);
- 'my last student' – basing the students' performance or level of development with a previous students. (adapted from Maclean with Lloyd, 2013, pp 133-5)

It is deeply worrying that in a profession like social work, which prides itself on its anti-oppressive values, research has highlighted discrimination against certain students, namely those from black and ethnic minority backgrounds, students with disabilities, and LGBT students.

Learning check
- What are three key issues you have learnt from this chapter?
- What are three key changes you will make in your practice, in terms of how you assess students in practice learning settings?
- How will you ensure your practice education approach is anti-discriminatory?

Chapter summary

This chapter has stressed that good practice education should look the same for all students, whether they are excellent, satisfactory, just about satisfactory, or are failing to meet the required standards. The research suggests that there are a number of reasons why practice educators might be reluctant to fail a student, and this is an important starting point in thinking about assessment of professional practice, which for all professions is a complicated business. Assessment regimes centred on competency models are in danger of simplifying the complexities of practice and promoting tick-box approaches; they may be biased and discriminatory, which, when coupled with high emotion, may result in poor assessment. Creative and critically reflective practice education, alongside a holistic approach to assessment, is therefore vital to ensure a high-quality learning experience for all students.

Further reading

Maclean, S. (2015a) *Social Work Theory Cards*, Lichfield: Kirwin Maclean Associates Ltd.

Maclean, S. (2015b) *Reflective Practice Cards: Prompt Cards for Social Workers*, Lichfield: Kirwin Maclean Associates.

Maclean, S. with Lloyd, I. (2013) *Developing Quality Practice Learning in Social Work: A Straightforward Guide for Practice Educators and Placement Supervisors*, Lichfield: Kirwin Maclean Associates Ltd.

Williams, S. and Rutter, L. (2015) *The Practice Educators Handbook* (3rd edn), London: Sage Publications, chapters 9, 10, 11.

WORKING CONSTRUCTIVELY WITH KEY STAKEHOLDERS IN SOCIAL WORK EDUCATION

> We see the student/tutor/practice teacher relationship as a power charged learning system where issues of status and authority are constantly at the fore and have an important influence on the quality of the placement experience. (Hackett and Marsland, 1997, p 49)

Introduction

This chapter focuses on working constructively with key stakeholders in social work education, namely the university and other key personnel, such as practice learning coordinators and social work tutors. The chapter has resonance for social work tutors, as the discussion highlights research that evidences difficult and angry relationships that may emerge when students are struggling on placement. The chapter goes on to examine research into tutors' experiences of working with struggling or failing students and their views of practice educators. The chapter considers the reasons for difficult relationships that sometimes emerge between the field and the academy, particularly when issues of struggling students arise. It encourages critical thinking about various forms of power and power differentials that might explain some of the conflict that emerges, and considers theories around defences against anxiety. Finally, the chapter asks reflective questions, with the overall aim of helping practitioners and tutors to work positively together.

Anger and blame

As documented in Chapter Three, the experience of working with failure can be incredibly emotionally painful. The chapter highlighted the stress and pain of failing a student (and of being failed). It is noted, however, that within the research the focus has tended to centre on practice educators' experiences at the expense perhaps of tutors' and, more importantly, students' experiences. Over the years, as an on- and offsite practice educator and social work tutor, I have observed how the pain of this experience not only affects the assessment process in adverse ways, as documented in Chapter Four, but also damages relationships between the field and the academy. It is the latter that the current chapter focuses on. The importance of constructive working relationships cannot be overstated, as a key facet of good practice in managing and supporting struggling students is to work together as a united front to ensure that assessment is fair and transparent and that the university's policies and procedures are enacted to ensure due process. This is important for upholding students' rights and for meeting gatekeeping responsibilities and duties to service users.

Practice educators

Finch (2010) documented practice educators' considerable anger not only towards the struggling or failing student, but also towards the tutor and, by implication, the university. Practice educators expressed narratives of 'us and them' and felt that universities did not like to fail students, although when pressed for evidence to support this view, practice educators maintained it was a 'feeling' or a 'sense' of something unspoken. Indeed, one practice educator spoke of a 'surreptitious discouragement of failure' by universities and another spoke of a feeling that 'red-brick universities' did not like to fail students as it was not good for their reputation. One practice educator was concerned about tutors colluding with students, in terms of a positive (biased) view of students appearing to detract from concerns about their placement. This practice educator, Martha, had raised serious concerns about her student at a placement meeting, but felt that the tutor could not move from the favourable view he had of the student. Martha comments:

"… we had such different, such difference of opinion that I really questioned my own judgment because I thought actually, this is somebody who has, you know, twenty years' experience of teaching, he's seen lots of students and I seem to be the only one who thinks there's a problem, he doesn't seem to think there is a problem with this student, he seems to think she is quite capable, intelligent and able to pass so I really questioned myself." (Finch, 2010, p 91)

The feeling that tutors always 'took the side' of the student, despite serious concerns being raised by practice educators, was raised in other accounts. One practice educator felt strongly that the university tutor had taken the side of the student when she raised some significant concerns that had resulted in an urgent meeting. The practice educator commented:

"So I went and had a meeting at the university after things had broken down to discuss it … they were only interested in what he [the student] had to say … and in fact when they sent a report, I wasn't prepared to sign the report they had sent because it didn't stress or recalled [sic] any of the concerns I had raised." (Finch, 2010, p 91)

The practice educator experienced further anger and frustration as her concerns had not been 'heard'. The practice educator had previously raised concerns with the university about why it had not been open at the outset about the student's medical issues. The practice educator felt that this raised questions about the suitability of the student's placement, given that the agency involved supported people with similar medical issues. The practice educator felt that the university tutor was engaging with the student as a service user rather than as a social work student and that her concerns about the student's practice and conduct were not adequately acknowledged or addressed by the university.

Such anger and frustration was a similar theme in other practice educators' accounts. Practice educators made angry comments about universities taking on inappropriate students just to fill the places on their programme. Some practice educators talked of having to deal with the 'university's mistakes', and concerns were raised, as in the incident described in the previous paragraph, that universities might be withholding vital or important information about students' learning or medical needs. One practice educator, for example, in Finch (2010) reported that it was only at the midway meeting, when the tutor asked her if she had read the access report about the student (which detailed the student's learning disability and support required), that she learnt that the student had dyslexia. At no point previously had the student or indeed the university disclosed this – a serious failure, given that the student was struggling. This type of incident was also found in research conducted in Italy, where some practice educators were concerned that the university had not disclosed vital information to them about students' health or disability needs (Finch and Poletti, 2013).

Schaub and Dalrymple (2011), in a study that aimed to explore the support needs of practice educators more generally, found that practice educators experienced feelings of isolation and felt unsupported by the university when issues of struggling or failing students emerged. Practice educators felt 'let down' by the university when such issues emerged, which caused feelings of resentment and anger. I would urge practice educators therefore to reflect on their experiences of social work tutors to date, as well as working relationships with other key university staff, namely placement coordinators. As always, be honest about your experiences and feelings, as it is only through acknowledging honestly our emotional reactions that we can make sense of them.

When I was a practice educator, I recall an incident where I experienced strong feelings about the social work tutor. At the midway meeting, as the tutor was going through my report, I felt that I was being scrutinised and under critical attack. I felt that the tutor, who was employed on a casual basis to undertake tutoring duties, was patronising, and that she was looking to find fault in my report. It felt like the focus was on me, rather than on the student. This was such an unpleasant emotional experience that I recall discussing it with the lecturers on the practice teachers' course I was undertaking at that time. In fact, recalling this incident now, some 16 years later, still provokes an uncomfortable emotional response. The quote at the beginning of this chapter talks perceptively of the learning system as 'power charged'. Perhaps what my encounter revealed all too starkly was how students feel in learning situations – under constant critical scrutiny. Or perhaps it was an example of mirroring from practice – a service user may have felt they were under critical attack and 'unfair scrutiny' from a student social worker, and this was played out in the meeting, a double mirroring from the service user to the student to me. There may have been other reasons. The student and I were very close in age, both relatively young, and the tutor was older; it could be that the tutor unconsciously adopted a critical parenting mode of interaction and that I responded in a rather childlike and defensive way. Perhaps the encounter reveals that while it is the norm for the practice educator and student to address issues of power imbalance, no such protocol exists between practice educators and social work tutors. In situations involving failing students (in the example I give the student was very strong indeed), such unacknowledged power struggles may have an adverse impact on both the assessment process and university procedure, as well as the relationships between the field and the academy. This leaves open the possibility of a failure to manage the situation in an open, fair and transparent way.

This is not to say that in the research discussed earlier (for example Finch, 2010; Schaub and Dalrymple, 2011; Finch and Poletti, 2013) all encounters with tutors were negative, but crucially, in terms of this book's overall theme of managing struggling students, practice educators observed that some tutors appeared more open to the possibility of students failing than others, and importantly, this openness to failure was experienced as supportive to practice educators.

Reflective exercise 5.1: Working with the university

- Overall do you feel you have a positive working relationship with the university? If yes, what makes the relationship positive? If no, why?
- What has been your experience to date of social work tutors?
- What feelings arise when you meet social work tutors at the initial placement learning meeting and midway meeting?
- Recall three specific encounters with a university tutor that have left you with strong emotions. Name those emotions and consider what the encounter represented or could have been about.

Tutors

There has been some limited research on social work tutors that highlights tutors' frustrations and at times anger towards practice educators who are perceived as failing fully to embrace their gatekeeping functions. Burgess et al (1998b) found that tutors felt that practice educators, rather than students, were a significant factor in placement breakdown or failure. Practice educators in these situations were typified as having poor communication skills, weak assessment ability and limited supervisory skills and, even more concerning, displaying unprofessional conduct. Finch's (2014) study noted the dissatisfaction felt by some tutors towards practice educators, not least when tutors felt practice educators were not open to the possibility of students failing, appeared to be unable to manage failing situations effectively, or indeed appeared reluctant to fail a student, despite significant concerns about the student's conduct and performance. Indeed, one social work tutor states:

"I think it was easier to pass than it was to fail them ... it's a combination of things, partly a bit laziness where they are, for whatever reason, reluctant to do the hard, extra work." (Finch, 2014, p 13)

Another tutor in the study commented on his frustration with some practice educators. He states:

"They're terrified of it because they think that they're being asked to judge and assess before they're ready to assess ... many of them want to be nice ... I think the niceness factor needs to be decreased and maybe they need to get more demanding." (Finch, 2014, p 13)

Interestingly, the same study revealed that tutors were critical not only of some practice educators, but also of some of their tutor colleagues, whom they felt were not managing failing situations in a helpful or appropriate manner. For example, some colleagues failed to respond to placement concerns in a timely fashion or did not follow procedures, which enabled students to successfully appeal against failed decisions; there were also claims of 'social working' struggling or failing students in a collusive manner. Concerns about tutors being reluctant to fail students is not new, however; an early but still relevant study by Brandon and Davies (1979), for example, found a reluctance by tutors to 'stand firm in the defence of standards' (p 51).

Reflective exercise 5.2: What I really think

Reflect on your response after reading the section on tutors, in particular the two quotes that were very critical of practice educators.

- What emotional reactions do these comments provoke?
- Do you think the comments are unfair? If so, why? If not, why?
- Why would the tutors make these somewhat blameworthy and angry comments about practice educators?

Understanding the dynamics of field–academy relationships

It is important to resist perpetuating difficult 'them and us' dynamics as a result of focusing too closely on research that documents frustrations and irritations, but rather to consider the reasons why difficult relations may emerge between the field and the academy. As discussed in Chapter Three, the emotional fallout from working with struggling or failing students may have a significant impact on relationships between the field and the academy. Two possible theoretical approaches for understanding these sometimes difficult relationships are explored in the next section, with the caveat, as always, that there are other theoretical explanations that could be equally relevant.

Power

The roles of both practice educator and social work tutor are complex and multifaceted, and both roles encompass a number of distinct and outwardly potentially conflicting requirements. If it is difficult for practice educators and social work tutors to manage such requirements, as research from across the professions has demonstrated, imagine how confusing it is for students to understand and make sense of the role of the practice educator and social work tutor. As discussed earlier, the dynamic between practice educator, tutor and student is a 'power charged learning relationship' (Hackett and Marsland, 1997, p 49), one where students will inevitably feel powerless, not least because the practice educator makes a recommendation at the end of the placement about whether the student is 'good enough'. Of course, students and practice educators are often unaware of the intricacies of university assessment regulations and the decision-making processes that follow the practice educator's recommendation of a pass or fail. It is likely, therefore, that students will see the practice educator as the only one responsible for the decision to pass or fail. As such, practice educators and tutors are imbued with both power and authority, real and imagined. Both parties must acknowledge their power, and the limits of their power, and use it in an appropriate, non-oppressive way.

Hawkins and Shohet (2010) propose a helpful model for considering the issue of power within supervisory roles, and this model could equally be applied to university personnel and practice education. The authors document three different 'sources' of power and authority. The first is 'role power' (2010, p 112), which refers to the power inherent in being a supervisor (or in this case a practice educator) and with it the so-called legitimate or justifiable power of being in this role and what it entails, namely assessment. Within this, there are less benign powers, referred to as coercive and reward or resources powers, so for example a coercive power may include compelling a supervisee to undertake a particular course of action in relation to a service user.

The second source of power arises from culture, that is, power that arises by virtue of being in a dominant group in terms of ethnicity, sexuality or gender, or cultural power gained from being a member of a particular profession – for example, a medical doctor has considerably more cultural power and authority than a social worker. The third source of power is what Shohet and Hawkins (2010) call 'personal power', in other words, power and authority that arise from someone's personality, authority or expertise over and above power resulting from role or cultural influences and status. Within this category, Shohet and Hawkins draw on the work of French and Raven (1959) to consider 'reverent power', whereby the supervisee wishes to identify with and become like the supervisor. This has some resonance with the notions of projective identification documented in Chapter Three, where at the benign end of the scale a supervisee (or a client) may want to emulate and occupy the mind of the supervisor (therapist or counsellor). We can also see parallels with Karpan's model of the drama triangle.

Consequently, in the practice educator–student–social work tutor triadic, there are competing and shifting power differentials at play. For example, the university tutor may be seen to hold the role power, while cultural power resides in one or other of the stakeholders. Given that students are increasingly adopting the role of consumers rather than participants of higher education, issues about personal power may also have an impact. Such roles, however, are nebulous and may shift significantly throughout the placement. As Hawkins and Shohet

(2010) so acutely observe, such shifting power differentials can make the task of supervision (or in this case practice education and tutoring) somewhat overwhelming and daunting. One practical way forward in developing constructive working relationships between the field and the academy is to be cognisant of the different sources of power and authority and consider how these may shift throughout the placement. Such an honest and reflective stance is, of course, taken for granted in terms of meeting standards based on anti-racist, anti-discriminatory and anti-oppressive values.

Reflective exercise 5.3: Understanding power and authority 1

- What role power is conferred on you? Is this role power constant or does it shift? When does it shift? How does that role power make you feel? How would others around you experience your role power?
- In what ways (if any) is cultural power conferred on you? How does this affect you and others around you?
- Do you feel you have personal power? If so, how does it manifest itself and what is the impact on those around you?

Now think about another key stakeholder in social work education – it could be a student, university tutor, practice educator or your line manager – and answer the questions below. It may be helpful to think about particular situations and people you have worked with previously.

Reflective exercise 5.4: Understanding power and authority 2

- What role power is conferred on that person? Is this role power constant or does it shift? When does it shift? How does that person's role power make you feel?
- In what ways is cultural power conferred on that person? How does this cultural power affect that person and others around them (including you)?
- Do you feel that person has personal power? If so, how does this manifest itself and what is the impact on you? How does that make you feel?

If you undertook this exercise again, with a different person in mind, would the outcome be different or similar? As explored in Chapter Three, how we respond to people we see in authority or those who have power over us may provoke an array of unconscious responses. It is these responses that we must identify and consider for own benefit, and use as a tool for understanding the states of mind of others we work with. An honest consideration of power is clearly part and parcel of working in an anti-oppressive and anti-discriminatory manner, and is crucial in adhering to the profession's value base.

Splitting and defences against anxiety

Having considered the power dynamics that emerge in all relationships, and honestly reflecting on our sources of power (or powerlessness), the discussion now moves on to consider a second theoretical perspective that may help us identify and understand the challenging triad dynamics that emerge in field–academy relationships. The concept of defences against anxiety, a Freudian notion later developed by Klein, is very relevant in understanding the emotional climate that appears to typify the process of working with a struggling student. Defences against anxiety manifest themselves in a number of ways, for example, splitting, denial, introjection, projection, aggression and acting out to name but a few (Frosh, 2012). Defences come into play, both consciously and unconsciously, when we feel under psychological attack or at risk of psychological harm, either real or perceived (Finch, 2016). The origins of defensive behaviours arise from early attachments formed in infancy and, as Winnicott notes, from our infantile experiences of 'failures and let-downs' (1958, p 61). Howe et al (1999) state that defence mechanisms originate from our efforts in infancy to 'cope with anxiety, abandonment, loss, conflict and emotional pain' (1999, p 93). It could therefore be argued that when working in a power-charged, emotionally painful learning situation, all stakeholders unconsciously engage in a range of defensive responses. Trevithick (2011) argues that in failing to recognise or address defensive responses that arise in ourselves, or failing to understand defensive responses in others, these defences 'distort our perceptions of reality' (2011, p 391).

The defensive concept of 'splitting' appears to be particularly relevant here, in terms of blaming, hostile and angry relationships that may develop between the field and the academy. Splitting is most associated with Klein and has complicated origins. In brief, splitting 'constitutes a phantasy whereby the subject may experience being split of, or else experience a splitting in the object that confronts him' (Grotstein, 1985, p 9). This defensive mechanism arises from infancy, whereby the infant must learn to integrate both the good object, the mother, with the bad object, the unresponsive mother (Fairbairn, 1994). Klein developed this further in her concept of the paranoid-schizoid and the depressive position – where one integrates these good and bad, internal and external objects (Hinshelwood, 1994). The impact of splitting, however, is that a person may be unable to bring together the good and the bad, and so views things in extremes, for example, the practice educator may view the student as good and the university as bad, or the student may view the practice educator as the bad object and the tutor as the good object. What is required is a move towards a Kleinian notion of a depressive position – one that integrates both good and bad objects, and helps us reflect more openly on the situation before us.

Reflecting on our tendency to split is important, not least to practice within anti-oppressive values and to ensure that immobilisation does not occur. Splitting tendencies reveal themselves in comments such as 'universities don't like to fail students' or 'universities are more concerned about bums on seats than the quality of students', comments that have often been made in the various practice education forums I have attended around the country over a number of years.

Ten essential building blocks for constructive working relationships

The discussion thus far leads us to identify ten essential building blocks for constructive working relationships:

1. Reflect constantly on power in all its forms, yours and others, and its consequences.
2. Be aware of the emergence of splitting dynamics.
3. Always follow the relevant processes.
4. Be clear about the purpose of your role.
5. Be clear about the responsibilities associated with your role.
6. Be clear about the roles of the other stakeholders.
7. Be clear about the responsibilities of other stakeholders.
8. Be honest about feelings that emerge and in particular acknowledge explicitly how painful it is to work with a struggling or failing student.
9. Have explicit but honest and 'courageous' conversations.
10. Remember that we all want the same thing – good-quality graduates.

Learning check

- What are three key issues you have learnt from this chapter?
- What are three key changes you will make in your practice, in terms of how you engage with and work with other stakeholders?
- How will you develop your practice with struggling or students at risk of failing as a result of this chapter?

Chapter summary

This chapter has highlighted research that suggests that there is sometimes conflict between the field and the university. In particular, this seems to emerge when there are placement difficulties generally, or when a student is struggling or at risk of failing a placement. The chapter has considered some of the underlying reasons for these conflicts. By being critically self-aware and aware of the possible sources of conflict, all stakeholders can work more constructively, openly and honestly together. This will ultimately ensure that the assessment procedure is fair, robust and transparent. In this way, the rights of students are guaranteed, and the potential users of social work agencies are protected from incompetent or even dangerous practitioners.

Further reading

Finch, J. (2014) '"Running with the fox and hunting with the hounds": social work tutors' experiences of managing students failing in practice learning settings', *British Journal of Social Work*, vol 45, no 7, pp 2124-41.

Finch, J. and Poletti, I. (2013) '"It's been hell." Italian and British practice educators' narratives of working with struggling or failing social work students in practice learning settings', *European Journal of Social Work*, vol 17, no 1, pp 135-50, DOI: 10.1080/13691457.2013.800026#.

Poletti, A. and Anka, A. (2013) '"They thought I wasn't good enough for social work practice"', *Journal of Practice Teaching and Learning*, vol 11, no 3, pp 17-35.

CONCLUSION

> Defining the minimum level of competent practice acceptable at qualification point is perhaps one of the most difficult tasks facing a practice educator. It is also one of the most important, as it decides who obtains a social worker qualification. (Sharp and Danbury, 1999, p 79)

Introduction

This last chapter offers a summary of the preceding chapters and attempts to offer some final comments about the inherent challenges of assessing practice in the field. The chapter begins with the contested nature of professions, before going on to consider the emotions of teaching and learning. The chapter also considers the implications for other contexts, such as supervision and management. Finally it considers whether there can ever be such a thing as a 'good fail'. The book ends by offering a succinct review of effective practice, namely the fifteen steps to work effectively and ethically with all students in practice learning settings.

The contested nature of professions

At the outset, this book set out the complicated landscape of social work education, and it is clear that other professions have equally fraught and contested debates in training students. These might include, for example, ideological concerns over the nature and purpose of that profession or indeed, the desirability of a competency approach to the task of assessment. It is important, however, that all practice educators are critically aware of their profession's historical context, not least so that they (and students) fully understand the norms of the current assessment regime and the reasons for its introduction. Some practice educators in the research informing this book have been shown to struggle to use assessment frameworks appropriately or effectively. This indicates a clear need to go beyond a tick-box approach to the task of assessment and use such frameworks in a holistic and thoughtful way, even though, as Finch and Poletti (2013) argue, they do not protect practice educators from the emotional pain associated with failing a student.

The emotions of teaching and learning

The book has emphasised the emotional aspects inherent in all teaching and learning relationships, and how our childhood experiences of early attachment figures (those in authority and in our formative education) continue unconsciously to influence our attitudes and expectations of learning relationships. Failing is therefore an incredibly emotive word and will conjure up all kinds of challenging associations, as many readers may have found out when engaging in the exercises in Chapter Four. As this book has highlighted, the danger of labelling a student as failing is problematic, not least in that all subsequent behaviour may be seen as evidence of failing rather than as normal development and learning.

Anti-discriminatory and anti-oppressive practice

The book has highlighted concerns about discrimination and oppression, not least evidence in the UK that certain groups of social work students are disproportionately represented in placement fails and progress more slowly through social work programmes. The book draws on research that reveals disturbing incidences of racism, for example, discriminatory attitudes towards Black African students' accents, accusations of dishonesty, and over-scrutiny of their performance (Tedam, 2014a, 2014b). Indeed, at the beginning of the book, I recounted the story of a former tutee, who was failed from a placement on very spurious, that is, discriminatory, and weak grounds, one of them being the student's pronunciation of 'foyer'. The book has also revealed issues around students' disabilities or learning needs not being adequately addressed on placement, or indeed not managed by universities themselves. Anecdotally this has resonance with me, as I have witnessed the failure to address dyslexic students' needs on placement and an unwillingness to conform to disability law in terms of 'reasonable adjustment'. These, of course, are not just placement issues; universities can be oppressive institutions, evidenced by the fact that while the numbers of black and minority ethnic students are increasing in all universities, their outcomes are considerably poorer than those of their white peers in terms of attainment and progression (Lenkeit et al, 2015; HEFCE, 2016).

From struggling to failing?

The book has focused on struggling students and those at risk of failing the placement. As stated at the outset, it is difficult to know how to refer to such students without seeming negative or appearing to pathologise. Indeed the term 'failing student' may suggest a recommendation that has already been made and cannot be retrieved. All students struggle with some things on placement, and the key is to know when those normal struggles and anxieties are in danger of developing into something more concerning that will need a more thoughtful approach with an accompanying intervention. At times, despite your best efforts and those of the university tutor, a student will be unable to progress in the manner required. As a practice educator, you will then be tasked with making a recommendation of a fail. You may also be asked to recommend whether you think another placement would be of benefit to the student, but I suggest you think carefully about this to ensure that your decision is not affected by your desire for the student to be successful. It is very easy to give students the benefit of the doubt – a phrase used in the Brandon and Davies (1979) study, but one that still feels very relevant.

The university then invokes a number of additional decision-making processes, sometimes in the form of a Practice Assessment Panel, usually staffed by a range of people including practice educators, service users and experts by experience. Any decisions made are scrutinised by an external examiner and the final decision is formally made at the university assessment or exam board. Students will have the opportunity to comment on the practice educator's report in a separate reflective statement that will be made available to the panel members and the external examiner. Students also have the opportunity to use the university's appeal procedure if they feel that due process has not been followed, or indeed if they feel their case meets the requirements of the appeal process. Despite these additional decision-making processes, it is not uncommon for practice educators to feel like a decision to fail is theirs alone and to feel quite burdened by this. As Eno and Kerr (2013) remind us, ensuring that the standards of the profession are maintained is an important function, and while the following consideration may be something of a cliché, you need to think carefully about giving a student the benefit of the doubt if you would not want them to work with a member of your family.

Unfinished business?

Practice educators are often not in a position to know the medium- or long-term outcome of any difficult decisions they have made to fail or pass a student. Indeed, practice educators interviewed for my doctoral research commented that they were not even informed about the immediate outcome, that is, whether or not the decision they had made was upheld by the university. If the student had to repeat the placement, were they successful? Of course, one could argue that it is none of their business, but not knowing may cause further guilt. Perhaps there is an accompanying need to make it 'all right' for the student, and not knowing feels like unfinished business. In an ideal world, a struggling or failing student might voluntarily withdraw from a professional programme, but in my experience, despite efforts by practice educators and university staff to counsel some students out of a programme of study, students have invested too much, financially and emotionally, to make that decision. Interestingly, social work education contrasts with that in nursing education, where traditionally there has been a high rate of attrition, with students voluntarily withdrawing from their programmes (Gidman, 2001). The question remains about why rates of voluntary withdrawal are so different in nursing compared with social work.

The notion of investment is important in this whole debate, as all stakeholders – students, tutors, placement coordinators, workforce development advisers and practice educators – will have 'invested' in the process in a number of ways, with time, energy, hope and, for students in particular, significant financial investment. One of the arguments therefore is that practice educators in particular, because of the emotional investment they make in their students, may internalise students' failings as their own. This, in turn, may make it even more difficult for practice educators to fail a student, as this may mean acknowledging their own failures to enable the student's learning and development.

The good fail?

This brings us to the question of whether there is any such thing as a 'good fail' or whether failing will always be imbued with negativity, pain and loss? Will there ever be a time when a student who fails their placement, and perhaps their course, will ever feel that the right decision was made? Eno and Kerr (2013) argue that there can be a 'good fail' and that there is a need not only to acknowledge the negativity around failing students, but to focus on the challenges of a robust assessment in a more positive way. They make a further important point that for some students the recommendation of a fail is experienced as a relief, as they may well be aware of their own shortcomings. Having someone else fail you, rather than make the decision to withdraw yourself, may also provide some relief for students. A psychodynamic view of this is that the students communicate through their behaviour or emotional state of mind the fact that they want to be failed. This, of course, feels counterintuitive, as failure is always associated with negativity. It may be worth thinking about your responses to the exercise on failure in Chapter Three. For many of us, I am sure, the failing experience turned out 'OK in the end' and there was some sort of resolution. For Eno and Kerr (2013), a good fail *is* possible and the features of a good fail include a robust but fair assessment, keeping the student informed at all times, working productively with the university, clarity around the students developmental needs in terms of omissions and commissions, and appropriate and sensitive support for practice educators by agencies and universities – in other words, many of the issues that this book covers.

Wider applications?

The hypotheses put forward in the preceding chapters, while aimed at social work practice education, have clear resonance for other professions with assessed practice learning requirements. They also resonate in terms of supervising and managing underperforming employees. The same emotional reactions are likely to emerge if you are managing an underperforming employee and the same fears and concerns will arise, such as fears of appeal processes and industrial tribunals. There is equally a need in these situations for line managers to have 'courageous conversations' with their supervisees, despite the reluctance and uncomfortable physical feelings that often accompany the need to give difficult feedback. Indeed, three American studies focusing on counselling psychologists revealed that supervisors were very reluctant to give negative feedback about perceived failings in their colleagues' practice (Goodman, 2004; Floyd et al, 1998; Hoffman, 2005). It is also important to reflect on how powerful our 'hopes' are, as, in the words of Coulshed (1980), the hope that 'competence and effectiveness [will] would blossom sometime in the future' (1980, p 17) is unrealistic, albeit understandable.

Fifteen steps to working effectively with (struggling) students on placement

Step 1: Stop, reflect and identify the feelings

The first step, which has been highlighted throughout this book, is to stop, think and reflect on the emotional dynamics at play. Challenging dynamics and accompanying emotional responses will always arise in teaching and learning relationships. These will also inevitably become magnified when students are struggling or failing. What are the feelings being experienced? What is the impact of those feelings on first, your practice, second, on the teaching and learning relationship, and third, on the student?

Step 2: Identify the source of the emotions and what is being communicated

Having identified some of the emotions and dynamics at play, the next step is to think about where they have arisen. Do the feelings experienced relate to the student's state of mind being projected on to you? What is being communicated by the student? Can you reflect this back to the student?

Step 3: Contain the emotional climate

You need to be able to withstand and take responsibility for containing the emotional dynamics at play in the relationship. The practice educator thus needs to regulate intolerable feelings and reflect them back in a more digested manner. The work of Ruch (2007) is very helpful in thinking about containment, and finding a safe reflective space to process the work is always helpful.

Step 4: Do not bury your head in the sand

Do not ignore issues as this will make the problem even more difficult to address in the long term. Ignoring an issue will not make it go away, so always address things as they arise.

Step 5: Do not over react

Linked to step 4 is the importance of not overreacting to normal or temporary placement blips, as these are to be expected. Avoid convening a concerns meeting at the first sign of a developmental need – this takes us back to step 3, the importance of containment.

Step 6: Collate the evidence

Whether the student is good, bad or indifferent, the importance of collating a wide variety of evidence to support your emerging hypotheses about the student's developmental needs as the placement progresses is always crucial. Assessment is thus an ongoing, formative process as well as a summative one when it comes to writing the report. Evidence is not just something to think about at the report stage.

Step 7: Avoid making assumptions

As Maclean with Lloyd (2013) cautioned in Chapter Four, the importance of avoiding assumptions during the assessment process is crucial. Do not assume that just because a student can do one thing they can necessarily do another. Similarly, do not assume that first impressions are the right ones, but do listen to your gut reactions and do not assume that all students will pass the placement.

Step 8: Give constructive, ongoing feedback

The need for ongoing assessment and constructive feedback is crucial. This ensures that the student is fully aware of areas that require further development and consideration. Constructive feedback should be owned, actionable, well timed, facilitative, clear and non-ambiguous, and should focus on two or three key areas. Always offer the student several suggestions about how they might tackle things differently. Think about the tone of your voice, your body language and how you come across, and pay attention to how the student reacts to the feedback. Go back to step 1 to step 3 if a student has an adverse reaction to the feedback given.

Step 9: Follow the process

Whilst it is recognised that some procedures are precautionary, process is nonetheless important in terms of protecting the student's right to a fair, transparent assessment. To ensure due process, always follow the procedures documented in the placement and programme handbooks, as they are there to protect everyone – students, practice educators and service users. As part of due process, you should highlight areas for development as soon as they arise, not at the placement meetings. A failure to follow due process may mean that your recommendation cannot be upheld and will result in a student successfully appealing a fail recommendation and having a further opportunity to repeat their placement, which is potentially detrimental to service users.

Step 10: Remember your role and responsibilities

Always keep in mind the myriad of functions within the overall practice educator role and accompanying responsibilities, and think about where they start and where they end.

Step 11: Avoid doing too much

Linked to step 8, there is a balance to be had between offering a supportive and facilitative approach to enable student growth and development and not doing too much for the student. Think about the balance of talk in supervision sessions with the student. If you can only hear your voice, something is amiss. It is the student's supervision/ practice teaching session, so they need to use it. If a student needs to read up on something, it is their responsibility to source that information, not yours. It is all too easy to get into rescuing mode, so always be alert to this possibility.

Step 12: Always employ adult learning principles

Linked to steps 8 and 9, always employ adult learning principles in your work with the student, as well as in the work around clarifying and managing expectations. Remind yourself of the underlying principles of adult learning notions, namely that the adult concerned should be self-directed in their learning.

Step 13: Do not internalise failing

If a student is struggling to make progress in a particular area, and you have tried hard to address those issues using creative techniques, try not to internalise the student's difficulties and make them your own. If you need to fail a student, this is not a reflection of you failing as a practice educator, but rather evidence of your abilities as a practice educator to uphold the required standards and act as a gatekeeper to the profession.

Step 14: Follow the same goals

It is always worth remembering that universities, practice educators and students all want the same thing, namely to educate students to become competent, ethical social work practitioners ready for their assessed and supported year in employment. Sometimes it is often worth reminding each other of this.

Step 15: Use the 'f' word judiciously

There is a balance to be struck between using and not using the 'f' word – namely the term fail – given that it is imbued with so much negativity. Do not refer to the student as a failing one, and avoid interpreting all of the student's behaviour and conduct as further evidence of 'failing'. On the other hand, you do need to inform the student that if they do not address particular areas, they are at risk of not meeting the requirements, which would result in a fail recommendation.

Final words

Working with failing or struggling students may cause unpleasant, difficult and confusing emotions, which can remind us unconsciously of our own previous experiences of failing. The importance for all of us to reflect on these difficult feelings and use them constructively to help students in their development and learning is clear, but if we need to fail a student on placement it should be managed in a reflective, 'calm' way, ensuring that due process has occurred.

References

Anglia Ruskin University (2013) 'Supporting the underachieving learner: a guide for mentors', available at: www.anglia.ac.uk/~/media/Files/NHS Mentors/Midwifery (FHSCE)/Mentor Updates/Midwifery Supporting the underachieving learner - guide for mentors.pdf (accessed 21 April 2016).

Bamford, T. (2015) 'Education: a contested landscape', Professional Social Work, March, available at http://cdn.basw.co.uk/upload/basw_43830-10.pdf (accessed 6 October 2016).

Basnett, F. and Sheffield, D. (2010) 'The impact of social work student failure upon practice educators', British Journal of Social Work, vol 45, no 7, pp 2124-41.

Beddoe, L. and Davys, A. (2016) Challenges in Professional Supervision, London: Jessica Kingsley.

Berne, E. (1967) Games People Play, London: Penguin.

Berne, E. (1977) Intuition and Ego States: The Origins of Transactional Analysis, New York, NY: Harper.

Bisman, C. (2014) Social Work: Value-Guided Practice for a Global Society, New York, NY: Columbia University Press.

Bogo, M., Regehr, C., Power, R. and Regehr, G. (2007) 'When values collide: field instructors' experiences of providing feedback and evaluating competence', The Clinical Supervisor, vol 26, no 1/2, pp 99-117.

Bower, M. (2005) 'Psychoanalytic theories for social work practice', in M. Bower (ed) *Psychoanalytic Theory for Social Work Practice*, Abingdon: Routledge.

Brandon, J. and Davies, M. (1979) 'The limits of competence in social work: the assessment of marginal students in social work education', *British Journal of Social Work*, vol 9, pp 295-347.

Brearly, J. (1991) 'A Psychodynamic Approach to Social Work', in J. Lishman (ed) *Handbook of Theory for Practice Teachers in Social Work*, London: Jessica Kingsley.

Brummer, N. (1998) 'Cross cultural student assessment: issues facing white teachers and black students', *Social Work Education*, 7, pp 3-6.

Burgess, R., Campbell, V., Phillips, R. and Skinner, K. (1998a) 'Managing unsuccessful or uncompleted placements', *Journal of Practice Teaching*, vol 1, no 1, pp 4-12.

Burgess, R., Philips, R. and Skinner, K. (1998b) Practice placements that go wrong. *Journal of Practice Teaching,* vol 1, no 2, pp 48-64.

Care Council for Wales (date unknown) 'Social work', available at www.ccwales.org.uk/qualifications-and-nos-finder/n/social-work (accessed 8 September 2016).

CCETSW (Central Council for Education and Training in Social Work) (1989) *Rules and Requirements for the Diploma in Social Work (Paper 30)*, London: CCETSW.

Clarkson, P. (1992) *Transactional Analysis Psychotherapy: An Integrated Approach*, London: Routledge.

Cleary, T. (2014) 'Weighing up the evidence: a review of the Narey and Croisdale-Appleby reports on social work education in *Community Care*', available at www.communitycare.co.uk/2014/07/15/weighing-quality-review-narey-croisdale-appleby-reports-social-work-education (accessed 6 October 2016).

Cleland, J., Arnold, R. and Chesser, A. (2005) 'Failing finals is often a surprise for the student but not the teacher; identifying difficulties and supporting students with academic difficulties', *Medical Teacher*, vol 27, no 6, pp 504-8.

Cleland, J., Knight, L., Rees, C., Tracey, S. and Bond, C. (2008) 'Is it me or is it them? Factors that influence the passing of underperforming students', *Medical Education*, vol 42, pp 800-9.

Cole, B.S. (1991) 'Legal issues related to social work program admissions', *Journal of Social Work Education*, vol 27, no 1, pp 18-24.

Cole, B.S. and Lewis, R. G. (1993) 'Gatekeeping through termination of unsuitable social work students: legal issues and guidelines', *Journal of Social Work,* vol 29, no 2, pp 150-59.

Cooper, A. (2005) 'Surface and depth in the Victoria Climbié Inquiry', *Child and Family Social Work*, vol 10, no 1, pp 1-9.

Cooper, A. and Lousada, J. (2005) *Borderline Welfare: Feeling and Fear of Feeling in Modern Welfare*, London: Karnac Books.

Coren, A. (1997) *A Psychodynamic Approach to Education*, London: Sheldon Press.

Cosis-Brown, H. (1998) 'Counselling', in R. Adams, L. Dominelli and M. Payne (eds) *Social Work: Themes, Issues and Critical Debates*, Basingstoke: Palgrave.

Coulshed, V. (1980) 'Why is placement failure so rare?', *Australian Social Work*, vol 33, no 4, pp 17-21.

Cowburn, M., Nelson, P. and Williams, J. (2000) 'Assessment of social work students: standpoint and strong objectivity', *Social Work Education*, vol 19, no 6, pp 627-37.

Croisdale-Appleby, L. (2014) *Revisioning Social Work Education: An Independent Review*, London: Department of Health, available at www.gov.uk/government/uploads/system/uploads/attachment_data/file/285788/DCA_Accessible.pdf.

Currer, C. and Atherton, K. (2008) 'Suitable to remain a student social worker? Decision making in relation to termination of training', *Social Work Education*, vol 27, no 3, pp 279-92.

DH (Department of Health) (2002) *Requirements for Social Work Training*, London: HMSO.

DH (2004) *First Annual Report – Practice Learning Taskforce*, London: HMSO.

Dingwall, R., Eekelaar, J. and Murray, T. (1983) *The Protection of Children: State Intervention and Family Life*, Oxford: Basil Blackwell:.

Doel, M. and Shardlow, S. (2002) 'Introduction: international themes in educating social workers for practice', in S. Shardlow and M. Doel (eds) *Learning to Practise Social Work: International Approaches*, London: Jessica Kingsley.

Duffy, K. (2003) 'Failing students: a qualitative study of factors that influence the decisions regarding assessment of students' competence in practice', Glasgow Caledonian University, available at www.nm.stir.ac.uk/documents/failing-students-kathleen-duffy. pdf (accessed 5 May 2016).

Dunworth, M. and Gordon, J. (2014) *Mapping of Standards in Social Work Education to the revised National Occupational Standards in Social Work*, Dundee: Scottish Social Care Council, available at www. sssc.uk.com/about-the-sssc/multimedia-library/publications/70-education-and-training/mapping-of-siswe-to-the-national-occupational-standards-2014 (accessed 8 October 2016).

Elman, N.S. and Forrest, L. (2007) 'From trainee impairment to professional competence problems: seeking new terminology that facilitates effective action', *Professional Psychology: Research and Practice*, vol 38, pp 501-9, doi:10.1037/0735-7028.38.5.501.

Eno, S. and Kerr, J. (2013) '"That was awful! I'm not ready yet, am I?" Is there such a thing as a good fail?', *Journal of Practice Teaching and Learning, Special Edition – Failing Students*, vol 11, no 3, pp 135-48.

Eraut, M. (1994) *Developing Professional Knowledge and Competence*, London: The Falmer Press.

Evans, D. (1999) *Practice Learning in the Caring Professions*, Aldershot: Ashgate.

Fairbairn, W.R.D. (1994) *Psychoanalytical Studies of Personality*, London: Routledge.

Fairtlough, A., Bernard, C. Fletcher, J., Ahmet, A. (2014) 'Black social work students' experiences of practice learning: understanding differential progression rates', *Journal of Social Work*, vol 14, no 6, pp 605-24.

Feasey, D. (2002) *Good Practice in Supervision with Psychotherapists and Counsellors*, London: Whurr.

REFERENCES

Finch, J. (2004a) 'Waiting for the light to go on', Assignment 2, Professional Doctorate in Social Work, Falmer: University of Sussex.

Finch, J. (2004b) 'A small-scale evaluation of tutor support given to practice teachers where there are concerns about failing or marginal students', Assignment 3, Professional Doctorate in Social Work, Falmer: University of Sussex.

Finch, J. (2005) *A Critical Analytical Study: The Assessment of Marginal and/or Failing Students in Placement*, Brighton: University of Sussex, doi: 10.13140/RG.2.1.5114.8567.

Finch, J. (2010) 'Can't fail, won't fail – why practice assessors find it difficult to fail social work students: a qualitative study of practice assessors' experiences of assessing marginal or failing social work students', DipSW thesis, University of Sussex, available at http://sro.sussex.ac.uk/2370 (accessed 1 January 2016).

Finch, J. (2013) *A Critical Exploration of Practice Assessment Panels: Participation, Power, Emotion and Decision Making in Relation to Failing Social Work Students*, York: Higher Education Academy, available at www.heacademy.ac.uk/resources/detail/resources/detail/disciplines/hsc/Social-Work-and-Social-Policy/A_critical (accessed 12 July 2015).

Finch, J. (2014) '"Running with the fox and hunting with the hounds": social work tutors' experiences of managing students failing in practice learning settings', *British Journal of Social Work*, vol 45, no 7, pp 2124-41.

Finch, J. (2015) Working with struggling or failing students in practice learning settings, Glasgow Caledonian University and Learning Network West Workshop, 13 November, available at www.westlearningnetwork.org.uk/images/GCU_November_2015_with_particpant_feedback_on.pdf (accessed 13 January 2016).

Finch, J. (2016) '"... it's just very hard to fail a student ..."': decision making and defences against anxiety – an ethnographic and practice-near study of practice assessment panels', *Journal of Social Work Practice*, doi: 10.1080/02650533.2016.1158156.

Finch, J. and Poletti, I. (2013) '"*It's been hell.*" Italian and British practice educators' narratives of working with struggling or failing social work students in practice learning settings', *European Journal of Social Work*, vol 17, no 1, pp 135-50, doi: 10.1080/13691457.2013.800026.

Finch, J. and Poletti, A. (2016) 'Italian and English practice educators' experiences of working with struggling or failing students in practice placements', in I. Taylor et al (eds) *Routledge International Handbook of Social Work Education*, London: Routledge.

Finch, J. and Schaub, J. (2015) 'Projective identification and unconscious defences against anxiety: social work education, practice learning and the fear of failure', in D. Armstrong and M. Rustin (eds) *Social Defences Against Anxiety: Explorations in a Paradigm*, London: Karnac Books.

Finch, J. and Taylor, I. (2013) 'Failing to fail? Practice educators' emotional experiences of assessing failing social work students', *Social Work Education (Special Edition, Field Education in Social Work)*, vol 32, no 2, pp 244-58.

Finch, J., Schaub, J. and Dalrymple, R. (2013) 'Projective identification and the fear of failing: making sense of practice educators' emotional experiences of failing social work students in practice learning settings', *Journal of Social Work Practice*, vol 28, no 2, pp 139-54.

Fisher, T. (1990) 'Competence in social work practice teaching', *Social Work Education*, vol 9, pp 9-25.

Floyd, M.R., Myszaka, M.T. and Orr, P. (1998) 'Licensed psychologists' knowledge and utilization of a state association colleague assistance committee', *Professional Psychology: Research and Practice*, vol 29, pp 594-98.

Forrest, L., Elman, N.S. and Shen Miller, D.S. (2008) 'Psychology trainees with competence problems: from individual to ecological conceptualizations', *Training and Education in Professional Psychology*, vol 2, no 4, pp 183-92.

French, J.R.P and Raven, B. (1959) 'The bases of social power', in D. Cartright (ed) *Studies in Social Power*, Ann Arbour, MI: Institute for Social Research.

REFERENCES

Frosh, S. (2012) *A Brief Introduction to Psychoanalytic Theory*, Basingstoke: Palgrave.

Furness, S. and Gilligan, P. (2004) 'Fit for purpose: issues from practice placements, practice teaching and the assessment of students' practice', *Social Work Education*, 23, pp 465-79.

Gidman, A. (2001) 'The role of the personal tutor: a literature review', *Nurse Education Today*, vol 21, no 5, pp 359-65.

Gizara, S.S. and Forrest, L. (2004) 'Supervisors' experiences of trainee impairment and incompetence at APA-accredited internship sites', *Professional Psychology: Research and Practice*, vol 35, no 2, pp 131-40.

Globerman, J. and Bogo, M. (2000) 'Changing times: understanding social workers' motivations to be field enstructors', *Social Work*, vol 48, no 1, pp 65-73.

Goodman, J.S. (2004) 'Feedback specificity, learning opportunities and learning', *Journal of Applied Psychology*, vol 89, no 5, pp 809-21.

Grotstein, J.S. (1985) *Splitting and Projective Identification*, New Jersey, Jason Aronson Inc.

Hackett, S. and Marsland, P. (1997) 'Perceptions of power: an exploration of the dynamics in the student-tutor-practice teacher relationship within child protection placements', *Social Work Education: The International Journal*, vol 16, no 2, pp 44-62.

Harvard Business Review (2016) *Difficult Conversations (HBR 20-Minute Manager Series)*, Boston: Harvard Business Review Press.

Hawkins, P. and Shohet, R. (2010) *Supervision in the Helping Professions* (3rd edn), Maidenhead: Open University Press.

HEFCE (Higher Education Funding Council for England) (2016) 'Higher education in England: key facts', available at www.hefce.ac.uk/media/HEFCE,2014/Content/Pubs/2016/201620/HEFCE2016_20.pdf (accessed 12 December 2016).

Hillen, P. (2013) *Enhancing Outcomes for Black and Minority Ethnic Social Work Students in Scotland*, Edinburgh: University of Edinburgh, available at www.iriss.org.uk/sites/default/files/enhancing_outcomes_bme_sw_students_final_report_sept_2013.pdf (accessed 30 October 2016).

Hinshelwood, R.D. (1994) *Clinical Klein*, London: Free Association Books.

Hoffman, M.A., Hill, C.E., Holmes, S.E. and Freitas, G.F. (2005) 'Supervisor perspective on the process and outcomes of giving easy, difficult, or no feedback to supervisees', *Journal of Counselling Psychology*, vol 52, no 1, pp 3-13.

Howe, D., Brandon, M., Hinings, D. and Schofield, G. (1999) *Attachment Theory, Child*

Maltreatment and Family Support, Basingstoke: Macmillan.

Hughes, L. and Heycox, K. (1996) 'Three perspectives on assessment in practice learning', in M. Doel and S. Shardlow (eds) *Social Work in a Changing World: An International Perspective on Practice Learning*, Aldershot: Ashgate, pp 85-102.

Humphrey, C. (2007) 'Observing students' practice (through the looking glass and beyond)', *Social Work Education*, vol 26, no 7, pp 723-36.

Humphries, B. (1998) 'Contemporary practice learning in social work', *Journal of Practice Teaching*, 1, pp 4-12.

Hunt, C. and West, L. (2006) 'Learning in a border country: using psychodynamic ideas in teaching and research', *Studies in the Education of Adults*, vol 32, no 2, pp 160-77.

Hussein, S., Moriarty, J. and Manthorpe, J. (2009) *Variations in Progression of Social Work Students in England: Using Student Data to Help Promote Achievement: Undergraduate Full-Time Students' Progression on the Social Work Degree*, London: Social Care Workforce Research Unit, King's College London and General Social Care Council.

Hussein, S., Moriarty, J., Manthorpe, J. and Huxley, P. (2008) 'Diversity and progression among students starting social work qualifying programmes in England between 1995 and 1998: a quantitative study', *British Journal of Social Work*, vol 38, no 8, pp 1588-609, doi: 10.1093/bjsw/bcl378.

Ilott, I. and Murphy, R. (1997) 'Feelings and failing in professional training: the assessor's dilemma', *Assessment and Evaluation in Higher Education*, vol 22, pp 307-16.

Ilott, I. and Murphy, R. (1999) *Success and Failure in Professional Education: Assessing the Evidence*, London: Whurr Publishers.

ITAA (International Transactional Analysis Association) (date unknown) 'International Transactional Analysis Association: key ideas', www.itaa-net.org/ta/keyideas.htm (accessed 17 January 2009).

Jayaratne, S., Brabson, H.V., Gant, L.M., Negba, B.A., Singh, A.K. and Chess, W.A. (1992) 'African-American practitioners' perceptions of their supervisors: emotional support, social undermining and criticism', *Administration in Social Work*, vol 16, pp 27-43.

Jervis, A. and Tilki, M. (2011) 'Why are nurse mentors failing to fail student nurses who do not meet clinical performance standards?', *British Journal of Nursing*, vol 20, no 9, pp 582-97.

Jones, S. and Joss, R. (1995) 'Models of professionalism', in M. Yeolly and M. Henkel (ed) *Learning and Teaching in Social Work: Towards Reflective Practice*, London: Jessica Kingsley.

Joseph, B. (2012) 'Projective identification: some clinical aspects', in E. Spillius and E. O'Shaughnessy (eds) *Projective Identification: The Fate of a Concept*, London: Routledge, pp 98-111.

Karpman, S. (1968) 'Fairy tales and script drama analysis', *Transactional Analysis Bulletin*, vol 7, no 26, pp 39-43.

Karpman, S. (1971) 'Options', *Transactional Analysis Journal*, vol 1, no 1, pp 79-87.

Kaslow, N.J., Forrest, L., Van Horne, B.A., Huprich, S.K., Pantesco, V.F., Grus, C.L., Miller, D. S.S., Mintz, L.B., Schwartz-Mette, R., Rubin, N.J., Elman, N.S., Jacobs, S.C., Benton, S.A., Dollinger, S.J., Behnke, S.H., Shealy, C.N. and Van Sickle, K. (2007) 'Recognizing, assessing, and intervening with problems of professional competence', *Professional Psychology: Research and Practice*, vol 38, no 5, pp 479-492.

Kearney, P. (2003) *Framework for Supporting and Assessing Practice Learning*, London: Social Care Institute for Excellence.

Kemshall, H. (1993) 'Assessing competence: scientific process or subjective inference? Do we really see it?', *Social Work Education*, vol 12, pp 36-45.

Knowles, M.S. (1970) *The Modern Practice of Adult Education: Pedagogy Versus Andragogy*, New York, Cambridge: The Adult Education Company.

Knowles, M.S., Holton E.F. and Swanson, R.A (2015) *The Adult Learner*, New York, NY: Routledge.

Lafrance, J., Lafrance, F.A. and Herbert, M. (2004) 'Gate-keeping for professional social work practice', *Social Work Education*, vol 23, pp 325-40.

Larocque, S. and Loyce, F. (2013) 'Exploring the issue of Failure to Fail in a Nursing Program', *International Journal of Nursing Education Scholarship*, vol 10, no 1, pp 1-8.

Lawson, S. (2010) 'Nurse mentors still failing to fail students', *Nursing Times*, available at www.nursingtimes.net/whats-new-in-nursing/acute-care/nurse-mentorsstill-failing-to-fail-students/5013926. article (accessed 17 July 2011).

Lenkeit, J., Caro, D. and Strand, S. (2015) 'Tackling the remaining attainment gap between students with and without immigrant background: an investigation into the equivalence of SES constructs', *Educational Research and Evaluation*, vol 21, no 1, pp 60-83.

Luft, J. and Ingham, H. (1955) *The Johari Window: A Graphic Model for Interpersonal Relations*, Berkeley, CA: University of California Western Training Lab.

Lymbery, M. (2003) 'Negotiating the contradictions between competence and creativity in social work education', *Journal of Social Work*, vol 3, pp 99-117.

Lyons, K. (1999) *Social Work in Higher Education*, Aldershot: Ashgate.

Maclean, S. (2011) *The Social Work Pocket Guide to Reflective Practice*, Lichfield: Kirwin Maclean Associates Ltd.

Maclean, S. (2012) *The Social Work Pocket Guide to Effective Supervision*, Lichfield: Kirwin Maclean Associates Ltd.

Maclean, S. (2015a) *Social Work Theory Cards*, Lichfield: Kirwin Maclean Associates Ltd.

Maclean, S. (2015b) *Reflective Practice Cards: Prompt Cards for Social Workers*, Lichfield: Kirwin Maclean Associates Ltd.

Maclean, S. (2017) *My CPD Journal*, Lichfield: Kirwin Maclean Associates.

Maclean, S. with Lloyd, I. (2013) *Developing Quality Practice Learning in Social Work: A Straightforward Guide for Practice Educators and Placement Supervisors*, Lichfield: Kirwin Maclean Associates Ltd.

Malihi-Shoja, L., Catherall, D., Titherington, J., Mallen, E., Hough, G. and the Comensus Writing Collective (2012) '"We aren't all winners": A discussion piece on "failure to fail" from a service user and carer perspective', *Journal of Practice Teaching and Learning*, vol 11, no 3, pp 8-16.

McLaughlin, K. (2008) 'The social worker versus the General Social Care Council: an analysis of care standards tribunal hearings and decisions', *British Journal of Social Work*, vol 40, no 1, pp 311-27.

Mitchell, J. (1991) *Selected Melanie Klein*, London: Penguin.

Moriarty, J., Manthorpe, J., Chauhan, B., Jones, G., Wenman, H. and Hussein, S. (2009) '"Hanging on a Little Thin Line": barriers to progression and retention', *Social Work Education: The International Journal*, vol 28, no 4, pp 363-79, doi: 10.1080/02615470802109890

Munro, E. (2010) *Munro Review of Child Protection Part One: A Systems Analysis*, London: Department for Education, available at www.gov.uk/government/uploads/system/uploads/attachment_data/file/175407/TheMunroReview-Part_one.pdf (accessed 18 September 2016).

Munro, E. (2011a) *Munro Review of Child Protection Interim Report: The Child's Journey*, London: Department for Education, available at www.gov.uk/government/publications/munro-review-of-child-protection-interim-report-the-childs-journey (accessed 18 September 2016).

Munro, E. (2011b) *Munro Review of Child Protection Final Report: A Child-Centred System*, London: Department for Education, available at www.gov.uk/government/publications/munro-review-of-child-protection-final-report-a-child-centred-system (accessed 18 September 2016).

Narey, M. (2014) *Making the Education of Social Work Consistently Effective*, London: Department for Education.

O'Hagan, K. (1996) 'Social work competence: an historical perspective', in K. O'Hagan (ed) *Competence in Social Work Practice: A Practical Guide for Professionals,* London: Jessica Kingsley.

Orme, J., MacIntyre, G., Green Lister, P., Cavanagh, K., Crisp, B., Hussein, S., Manthorpe, J., Moriarty, J., Sharpe, E. and Stevens, M. (2009) 'What (a) difference a degree makes: the evaluation of the new social work degree in England', *British Journal of Social Work,* vol 39, no 1, pp 161-78.

Owens, C. (1995) 'How the assessment of competence in DipSW is changing the culture of practice teaching', *Social Work Education,* vol 14, pp 61-8.

Parker, J. (2010) 'When things go wrong! Placement disruption and termination: power and student perspectives', *British Journal of Social Work,* vol 40, no 3, pp 983-99.

Parrott, L. (1999) *Social Work and Social Care,* London: Routledge.

Payne, M. (2005) *Modern Social Work Theory (3rd edn),* Basingstoke: Palgrave.

Phillipson, J. (2006) *Planning and delivering practice learning in local authorities: key messages, Practice Learning Taskforce,* Leeds: Skills for Care, available at: www.scie-socialcareonline.org.uk/planning-and-delivering-practice-learning-in-local-authorities-key-messages/r/a11G00000017vCsIAI (accessed 20 January 2017).

Poletti, A. and Anka, A. (2013) '"They thought I wasn't good enough for social work practice"', *Journal of Practice Teaching and Learning,* vol 11, no 3, pp 17-35.

Powell, F. (2001) *The Politics of Social Work,* London: Sage Publications.

Pritchard, J. (1995) 'Supervision or practice teaching for students', in J. Pritchard (ed) *Good Practice in Supervision,* London: Jessica Kingsley.

Proctor, A.K. (1993) 'Tutors' professional knowledge of supervision and the implications for supervision practice', in J. Calderhead and P. Gates (eds) *Conceptualizing Reflection in Teacher Development,* London: The Falmer Press.

Raymond, G.T. (2000) 'Gatekeeping in field education', in P. Gibbs and E.H. Blakely (eds) *Gatekeeping in BSW Programs,* New York, NY: Colombia University Press.

Reamer, F.G. (2006) *Social Work Ethics and Values (3rd edn)*, New York, NY: Columbia University Press.

Robertson, J. (2013) 'Addressing professional suitability in social work education: results of a study of field education coordinators' experience', *Journal of Practice Teaching and Learning*, vol 11, no 3, pp 3-7, doi: 10.1921/1802110301.

Royse, P. (2000) 'The ethics of gatekeeping', in P. Gibbs and E.H. Blakely (eds) *Gatekeeping in BSW Programs*, New York, NY: Colombia University Press.

Ruch, G. (2000) 'Self and social work: towards an integrated model of learning', *Journal of Social Work Practice*, vol 14, no 2, pp 99-112.

Rutkowski, K. (2007) 'Failure to fail: assessing nursing students' competence during practice placements', *Nursing Standard*, vol 22, no 13, pp 35-40.

Salzberger-Wittenberg, I., Williams, G. and Osborne, E. (1983) *The Emotional Experience of Learning and Teaching*, London: Karnac Books.

Samec, J.R. (1995) 'Shame, guilt and trauma: failing the psychotherapy candidate's clinical work', *The Clinical Supervisor*, vol 13, no 2, pp 1-17.

Sawdon, D.T. (1986) *Making Connections in Practice Teaching*, London: National Institute for Social Work.

Schaub, J. (2015) 'Issues for men's progression on English social work honours and postgraduate degree courses', *Social Work Education*, doi/full/10.1080/02615479.2014.997698.

Schaub, J. and Dalrymple, R. (2011) '"She didn't seem like a social worker": practice educators' experiences and perceptions of assessing failing social work students on placement', available at www.swapbox.ac.uk/1151 (accessed 1 December 2012).

Schaub, J. and Dalrymple, R. (2013) 'Surveillance and silence: new considerations in assessing difficult social work placements', *Journal of Practice Teaching and Learning*, vol 11, no 3, pp 79-97.

Schraer, R. (date unknown) 'Criticisms of social work education review are "patent nonsense", says Narey: Martin Narey hits back against criticism that his report into social work education is not evidence-based', available at www.communitycare.co.uk/2014/07/08/criticisms-social-work-education-review-patent-nonsensesays-narey (accessed 17 August 2015).

Segal, J. (1992) *Melanie Klein*, London: Sage Publications.

Shapton, M. (2006) 'Failing to fail: is the assessment process failing the caring profession?', *Journal of Practice Teaching and Learning*, vol 7, no 2, pp 39-54.

Shardlow, S. and Doel, M. (1996) *Practice Learning and Teaching*, Basingstoke: Macmillan.

Sharp, M. and Danbury, H. (1999) *The Management of Failing DipSW Students: Activities and Exercises to Prepare Practice Teachers for Work with Failing Students,* Aldershot: Ashgate.

Skinner, K. and Whyte, B. (2004) 'Going beyond training: theory and practice in managing learning', *Social Work Education*, vol 23, no 4, pp 365-81.

Smith, E.R. and Mackie E.D.M. (2000) *Social Psychology (2nd edn)*, Philadelphia, PA: Psychology Press.

Spillius, E., Milton, J., Garvey, P. and Couve, C. (2011) *The New Dictionary of Kleinian Thought*, London: Routledge.

Sunderland, M. and Engleheart, P. (1997) *Draw on Your Emotions*, Milton Keynes: Speechmark Publishing Ltd.

SWRB (Social Work Reform Board) (2010) *Building a Safe and Confident Future: One Year On—Progress Report from the Social Work Reform Board*, London: Department of Education, available at: www.education.gov.uk/publications/standard/publication Detail/Page1/DFE-00601-2010 (accessed 23 May 2012).

SWTF (Social Work Task Force) (2009) *Facing up to the Task: The Interim Report of the Social Work Task Force*, London: Department of Health and Department for Schools, Children and Families, available at http://webarchive.nationalarchives.gov.uk/20130401151715/http://www.education.gov.uk/publications/eOrderingDownload/DCSF-00753-2009.pdf (accessed 19 September 2016).

Syson, L. and With Baginsky, M. (1981) *A Study of Placements in Courses Leading to the CQSW,* London: CCETSW.

Tedam, P. (2014a) 'When failing doesn't matter: a narrative inquiry into the social work practice learning experiences of Black African students in England', *International Journal of Higher Education,* vol 3, no 1, pp 136-45.

Tedam, P. (2014b) 'Enhancing the practice learning experiences of BME students: strategies for practice education', *Journal of Practice Teaching and Learning,* vol 12, no 2/3, pp 146-57.

Terry, P. (2008) 'Ageism and projective identification', *Psychodynamic Practice,* vol 14, no 2, pp 155-68.

TOPSS (Training Organisation for the Personal Social Services) (2002) *National Occupational Standards for Social Work,* Leeds: TOPSS.

Trevithick, P. (2011) 'Understanding defences and defensiveness in social work', *Journal of Social Work Practice: Psychotherapeutic Approaches in Health, Welfare and the Community,* vol 25, no 4, pp 389-412.

UK Parliament (2012) 'Health Committee: Written evidence submitted by The College of Social Work', available at www.publications. parliament.uk/pa/cm201012/cmselect/cmeduc/1630/1630we03. htm (accessed 16 September 2016).

Vacha-Haase, T., Davenport, D.S. and Kerewsky, S.D. (2004) 'Problematic students: gatekeeping practices of academic professional psychology programs', *Professional Psychology: Research and Practice,* vol 35, no 2, pp 115-22.

Wayne, J., Bogo, M. and Raskin, M. (2013) 'Field education as the signature pedagogy of social work education', *Journal of Social Work Education,* vol 46, no 3, pp 327-39.

Walker, J., McCarthy, P., Morgan, W. and Timms, N. (1995) *In Pursuit of Quality: Improving Practice Teaching in Social Work,* Newcastle Upon Tyne: Relate Centre for Family Studies.

Walker, J., Payne, S., Smith, P. and Jarrett, N. (2004) *Psychology for Nurses and the Caring Professions,* Maidenhead: Open University Press.

Williams, S. and Rutter, L. (2015) *The Practice Educator's Handbook (3rd edn),* London: Sage Publications.

Williamson, H., Jefferson, R., Johnson, S. and Shabbaz, A. (1985) *Assessment of Practice: A Perennial Concern: A Study of Current Methods, Skills and Knowledge Used by Practice Teachers to Evaluate the Competence of Social Work Students*, Cardiff: School of Social and Administrative Studies, University of Wales College of Cardiff, Centre for Social Work Studies.

Winnicott, D.W. (1958) *Collected Papers: Through Paediatrics to Psychoanalysis*, London: Tavistock Clinic.

Youell, B. (2006) *The Learning Relationship: Psychoanalytic Thinking in Education*, London: Karnac Books.

Zuchowski, I., Savage, D., Miles, D. and Gair, S. (2013) 'Decolonising field education: challenging Australian social work praxis', *Advances in Social Welfare and Social Welfare Education*, vol 15, no 1, pp 47-62.

Index